PRINCIPLES OF TEACHING

Dr. Bill Smallman

TRUSTpages Series

CreateSpace 2018

T eacher **R** esources **U** nfolding **S** cripture **T** ruth	The **TRUST** **Series** of adult Bible study books is designed for Sunday school teachers, small group leaders, and similar teachers of the Bible. Each book covers a specific part of the Bible or doctrine with conservative Christian teaching.

These ABF teacher training notes are original with the author except for quoted material which credits the authors of such comments. He is responsible for opinions expressed herein. These lessons are intended to help enable teachers of adult Bible classes of any sort to function well and use sound methodology.

The cover photo from www.123RF.com shows adults enjoying study.

Bible quotations are from the King James Version in the public domain, the New King James Version of the Bible © 1982 Thomas Nelson Publishers, used within their kindly permitted parameters., or from the English Standard Version © 2001 Crossway Publishers within their kindly permitted parameters, or the author's own translation of phrases from the Greek text.

Printed in the United States of America by CreateSpace® and available through Amazon.Com and other fine booksellers.

Principles of Teaching

By Dr. Bill Smallman

ISBN-10: 1725094266
ISBN-13: 978-1725094260

WHAT IS THIS?

These notes are NOT a college textbook on teacher training. They are lessons for lay persons teachers of Bible classes for adults, intended to provoke both understanding and application in our lives. They can be used for self-teaching in solo reading, in classes for prospective teachers, or for refresher courses for those already teaching. Teachers are constant learners who keep overflowing to other learners.

Due to time constraints, the explanations of Bible verses or educational principles are necessarily brief, and are designed for laypersons. Since we focus on methods, a class for training teachers must involve more than lecture so it will model what else the future teachers are to do in class.

You are welcome to use my words in your teaching, or you can talk through the material in your own words. These TRUSTpages Series books are simply a resource to help you teach the content, background, flow, and application of the Bible to in YourChurch in YourTown.

YOU can follow these notes as best suits your needs, used...
- ❖ For teaching as students listen and discuss,
- ❖ For your personal development

OPEN your BIBLE as you read the Bible verses quoted. I did not often include the Bible text in these lessons.

PRINCIPLES OF TEACHING

Teaching Adults The Bible

1

WHO IS A TEACHER?

An Adult Bible Fellowship teacher is to facilitate the learning and application of the Bible, book by book and doctrine by doctrine, by all who are in that class. In these lessons we will use the term "Adult bible Fellowship" or ABF, where "Sunday school" or "Bible Academy" or other similar terms might be in use in various churches. Apply the term accordingly.

The teacher is a model of the lifestyle taught in the content of the lessons, whether they are book studies, doctrine studies, or Christian life studies. He or she is an encourager, a teacher, and a discipler. He or she is also a conscious extension of the pastoral ministries of the church to its own people and others in their circles of influence.

It is easy to assert that the most important element of the ABF class is the Bible. In the sense of final authority that is certainly true. But people have Bibles at home that they quite ignore. The function of the Bible class is to get that Bible into the minds and lifestyles of its members. In that sense, the most important element in the ABF class is its teacher. You! Let's think about characteristics.

QUALIFICATIONS

TEAM PLAYER. The teacher is a **team player.** An ABF teacher shall be a member of the church, committed to its purpose, programs and leadership, as a loyal member of the larger ministry team. This implies full agreement with, and deep understanding of, the Articles of Faith of the church. It is normal to require that ABF teachers, as part of the teaching ministry, be members of that church.

There is no financial remuneration for ABF teachers. An ABF teacher is a committed **VOLUNTEER** in this vital ministry as a servant of Christ. The class is a conscious supplement to the preaching ministry of the pastor.

SELF-DRIVEN LEARNER. The teacher is a **FELLOW-LEARNER**, one who is motivated to keep learning the Scriptures, applying them to life, and communicating to others what is learned. This does not call for specific academic background, though every ABF teacher should have basic training in inductive Bible study (Huh? See Chapter 4) and Andragogy. (What? See Chapter 8.) He or she will seek access to resources for each specific study series undertaken, including the Church Library. Some Bible college or Bible institute courses would clearly enrich the teacher's own knowledge of Scripture and ministry, but is often not the case. The social maturity of the teacher shall be appropriate for the age or group targeted by each class. Where there are options for adult classes, people are more often drawn to the teacher than to the subject matter for a given period of time.

COMMUNICATOR. The teacher is a **communicator,**

> ➢ **able to organize** his or her thoughts about the Bible and other lesson content,

> ➤ **able to express** concepts and principles concisely and convincingly,
> ➤ **able to illustrate** biblical principles from ordinary life situations, and
> ➤ **eager to interact** with students and draw out their insights within the range of the lesson subject matter and its practical application. All this without feeling attacked, threatened, or defensive about the lesson.

He or she can employ a variety of teaching modes: lecture, discussion, buzz groups, object lessons, storytelling, etc., and knows the use of appropriate instructional media. We will see more about methods later on.

MODEL. The teacher lives out in his or her lifestyle the biblical principles that are explained in the classroom. This is not perfection, but a consistent pattern of displaying the character traits and behaviors that are being taught as biblical. When the lifestyle of the teacher is known to be in harmony with the teaching, the lessons have far more impact. They are a reality for the teacher that students can emulate.

RESPONSIBILITIES

The ABF teacher will diligently study the lesson material with a view toward its impact on his or her own spiritual life development, normally going beyond the basic resources for teachers in a quarterly to additional study materials. As a teacher looks forward to coming lessons or lesson series, it is wise to seek out resource materials that may be applicable at later times. Look forward to coming classes and topics.

> ➤ The teacher is a **STUDENT**, and will carefully prepare and teach a lesson each week, whether following a structured quarterly or developing his or her own

lesson material from other sources, with handouts or other appropriate media for student use.

➤ It is expected that the teacher will be **FAITHFUL**, present every week apart from scheduled absences for which advance notice is given to the co-teacher or other responsible persons, apart from emergencies or illness.

➤ The teacher is a **DISCIPLER**, and will develop a pastoral sense of responsibility for the spiritual care of the class. This may well include regular prayer, expressions of support in times of need, hospital or home visits as needed, and motivating class members to look out for one another.

➤ The teacher is an **EVANGELIZER**, and will see to it that every member of his or her class has been offered the free gift of salvation. He or she will personally approach any class members about whom there is any doubt of their salvation to share the gospel with compassion and patience. Such names can also be given to the ABF Recorder for follow-up by a visitation team.

➤ The teacher will be **ACCURATE**, overseeing the keeping of class records of attendance and the handling of offerings taken up by the class, normally by having the class name a secretary and treasurer, and will see to the follow-up of absentees. The records system of each class will dovetail with the overall records system of the ABF and church.

➤ The teacher will encourage every member of the class to participate in a home life group, as a small group Bible study for further fellowship, outreach, and accountability to others. The types of small group fellowship depend on what the church offers in its own menu of spiritual growth opportunities.

TENURE

The position of ABF teacher is intended to be indefinite. In practicality, it continues as long as both the class and the teacher are willing to continue, since either party could end the relationship.

Having a co-teacher facilitates the long-range ministry of an ABF teacher since there are regular times of non-teaching to prevent fatigue. A regular teacher could take a "furlough" for a month or a quarter, or simply schedule certain Sundays off, whether he or she attends that class or visits another class.

RELATED ACTIVITIES

The social activities of each ABF class are set up at the discretion of the class with an eye on the larger calendar of the church, to allow maximum participation in appropriate church-wide activities as well as its own outside ventures.

The teacher is a **TRAINER**, and will cooperate in the development of a co-teacher, whether for shared teaching of all classes, or teaching in rotation, or a stated substitute. Ideally, every teacher will have a partner in that ministry to ensure continuity and prevent burnout. ABF teachers should occasionally visit one another's classes for rest, observation of other teachers, and interaction.

Each teacher will participate in the scheduled meetings of ABF teachers for mutual encouragement, joint planning, and discussion of the particular needs and schedules of classes in relation to the overall church calendar. Such meetings are up to the Superintendent, by whatever title.

AUTHORITY

All who teach the Bible serve under the authority of the Scriptures, and serve within the network of ministries of the church. No ABF class is an autonomous ministry. It is an element in the Adult Ministries of YourChurch as a whole under the direction that ministry team, the guidance of the pastor, the authority of the congregation, and the overarching Lordship of Christ.

The authority of the teaching material in an ABF class is the authority of the Word of God, not of the teachers.

ABF classes are free to select the subject matter they wish to study, in harmony with the doctrinal position of the church, subject to approval by the ABF Superintendent. Study materials will be provided by the church, whether regular ABF curricular quarterlies or other basic books used as a student text for lesson material. If ABF teachers have the church purchase other study books for his or her use as a teacher, they shall be turned in to the church library when that study series is completed. Other teachers can use them as well. When some teachers prepare original lesson material for their own class, it may be fitting to keep a copy of that in the ABF files for possible use by other teachers.

ACCOUNTABILITY

A teacher of the Scriptures is ultimately accountable to their Author, both as to the accuracy of lesson content and the obedient lifestyle of the teacher.

The ABF teacher is immediately **ACCOUNTABLE** to the members of the class as to the quality of the teaching, the level of interest maintained, the direction of ministering for the good of the students, and conformity to the doctrines and principles of the church itself. A class which is dissatisfied with its teacher should communicate that to the ABF Superintendent for follow-up, leading either to corrective counsel and training, or removal from the teaching post.

There could be an annual review by the ABF Superintendent, allowing the class to voice its desire for the teacher(s) to continue on. The more practical approach is to assume that things are going well as long as there are no complaints that reach the ABF administration.

Being an ABF teacher at YourChurch is a privilege, not a right.

SUMMARY: So far, a teacher has certain attributes we discussed:

Team player, volunteer, fellow-learner, communicator, model of values, faithful, discipler, evangelizer, accurate, trainer, accountable.

WHAT DOES IT MEAN TO "TEACH" ??

➤ Get what is in the teacher's mind **into the minds of the students**.
  - ...without attempting a brain transplant.
  - **Attitude** as well as information: Students should enjoy the prospect of usefulness of the material in their real-life experience. "I want to be like that teacher."
  - Still, they shall be able to **think independently** about it all, disagree at times with what the prof says, or how s/he feels about it, and free to raise questions in class in a civil manner.
➤ **Motivate** the students to learn and put into practice

what is intended for that class.

➤ Guide the **incorporation** of that subject matter into the LIFESTYLE of each student.
  o There is no app for that since the reorganized info would still be outside the mind of the student. The student must want to conform to God's truth.

I wrote in 2001,

> A **ministry trainer** is a fellow-learner who models the ministry and explains how and why to perform it by creating an environment and providing resources which facilitate appropriate changes in the knowledge, motivation, and behavior of the ministry candidate, all from the vantage of greater experience, knowledge, and success. (Smallman, 2001, 23)

The Bible speaks of *teaching* or *teach* over 200 times. Here are a few of those, some in formal school settings, some at home, some on the receiving end. (Thanks to www.BibleGateway.org)

REF	VERSE	COMMENT
Exodus 4:12	Now therefore, go, and I will be with your mouth and teach you what you shall say	God is the ultimate source of our spiritual teaching.
Exodus 18:20	And you shall teach them the statutes and the laws, and show them the way in which they must walk and the work they must do.	Knowledge is to become lifestyle.
Ezra 7:10	For Ezra had prepared his heart to seek the Law of the Lord, and to do it, and to teach statutes and ordinances in Israel.	Teaching calls for preparation of heart and mind.
Job 27:11	I will teach you about the hand of	Deep truth is

	God; What is with the Almighty I will not conceal.	available to all people.
Psalm 25:4	Show me Your ways, O Lord; Teach me Your paths.	God will teach willing disciples.
Psalm 25:8	Good and upright is the Lord; Therefore He teaches sinners in the way.	Evangelism is teaching the Good News.
Psalm 32:8	I will instruct you and teach you in the way you should go; I will guide you with My eye.	Teaching leads to wise lifestyle.
Psalm 119:66	The earth, O Lord, is full of Your mercy; Teach me Your statutes.	Creation affirms the truth of the written Word.
Psalm 132:12	If your sons will keep My covenant And My testimony which I shall teach them, Their sons also shall sit upon your throne forevermore.	Good teaching brings along the next generation of teachers for God.
Proverbs 9:9	Give instruction to a wise man, and he will be still wiser; Teach a just man, and he will increase in learning.	Everyone is to grow. We are never perfect.
Isaiah 2:3	Many people shall come and say, "Come, and let us go up to the mountain of the Lord, To the house of the God of Jacob; He will teach us His ways, And we shall walk in His paths." For out of Zion shall go forth the law, and the word of the Lord from Jerusalem.	Learning is a shared experience, at God's House and along the way.
Isaiah 28:26	For He instructs him in right judgment, His God teaches him.	God's teaching is good for all people.
Jeremiah 31:34	No more shall every man teach his neighbor, and every man his brother, saying, 'Know the Lord,' for they all shall know Me, from the least of them to the	When the New Covenant is in effect, people will have a Teacher within their

	greatest of them, says the Lord. For I will forgive their iniquity, and their sin I will remember no more."	spirits.
Matthew 4:23	And Jesus went about all Galilee, teaching in their synagogues, preaching the gospel of the kingdom, and healing all kinds of sickness and all kinds of disease among the people.	Teaching, preaching, and healing go well together. It is all uplifting.
Matthew 5:19	Whoever therefore breaks one of the least of these commandments, and teaches men so, shall be called least in the kingdom of heaven; but whoever does and teaches them, he shall be called great in the kingdom of heaven.	Teachers have heavy responsibility before God.
Mark 6:2 [Luke 4:32]	And when the Sabbath had come, He began to teach in the synagogue. And many hearing Him were astonished, saying, "Where did this Man get these things? And what wisdom is this which is given to Him, that such mighty works are performed by His hands!	Jesus asserted His own authority, not merely quoting the sages of the ages.
Mark 6:6	And He marveled because of their unbelief. Then He went about the villages in a circuit, teaching.	Facts provoke faith.
Mark 12:14	When they had come, they said to Him, "Teacher, we know that You are true, and care about no one; for You do not regard the person of men, but teach the way of God in truth. Is it lawful to pay taxes to Caesar, or not?	Beware idle compliments that are a setup for a challenging question.
Luke 7:40	And Jesus answered and said to him, "Simon, I have something to	Disciples are students, always

	say to you." So he said, "Teacher, say it."	ready to hear the Master's teaching
John 13:13	You call Me Teacher and Lord, and you say well, for so I am.	He acknowledged that their honor was due Him.
John 13:14	If I then, your Lord and Teacher, have washed your feet, you also ought to wash one another's feet.	Jesus modeled the servant attitude as the highest form of living.
John 14:26	But the Helper, the Holy Spirit, whom the Father will send in My name, He will teach you all things, and bring to your remembrance all things that I said to you.	The Spirit authored the New Testament, and now He helps us understand it.
Acts 5:28	saying, "Did we not strictly command you not to teach in this name? And look, you have filled Jerusalem with your doctrine, and intend to bring this Man's blood on us!"	They would not stop teaching until all had heard of Jesus' work.
Acts 5:42	And daily in the temple, and in every house, they did not cease teaching and preaching Jesus as the Christ.	Teaching can be evangelistic, aimed at non-believers.
Acts 15:35	Paul and Barnabas also remained in Antioch, teaching and preaching the word of the Lord, with many others also.	The Purpose of the church is teaching and worship.
Acts 28:31	preaching the kingdom of God and teaching the things which concern the Lord Jesus Christ with all confidence, no one forbidding him.	Even while under house arrest Paul kept on teaching about the Person and Work of Jesus Christ.
1 Corinthians 2:13	These things we also speak, not in words which man's wisdom teaches but which the Holy Spirit teaches, comparing	The Holy Spirit's teaching was to specific men, inspiring the

	spiritual things with spiritual.	written Words of God.
1 Corinthians 4:17	For this reason I have sent Timothy to you, who is my beloved and faithful son in the Lord, who will remind you of my ways in Christ, as I teach everywhere in every church.	Those we have taught are the next generation of teachers of the Word.
Hebrews 5:12	For though by this time you ought to be teachers, you need someone to teach you again the first principles of the oracles of God; and you have come to need milk and not solid food.	There are levels of teaching appropriate for levels of spiritual maturity, not measured in mere time.
James 3:1	My brethren, let not many of you become teachers, knowing that we shall receive a stricter judgment.	James reminds teachers of Jesus' recognition that being a teacher is a weighty responsibility.
2 Peter 2:1	But there were also false prophets among the people, even as there will be false teachers among you, who will secretly bring in destructive heresies, even denying the Lord who bought them, and bring on themselves swift destruction.	Not all religious teaching is true, that is, in harmony with the Word of God.
1John 2:27	But the anointing which you have received from Him abides in you, and you do not need that anyone teach you; but as the same anointing teaches you concerning all things, and is true, and is not a lie, and just as it has taught you, you will abide in Him.	The ultimate authority is not the human teacher but the Holy spirit. Truth comes from God, not teachers. Discern truth!

We tend to focus on the ministries of Jesus Christ related to his ATONEMENT since He came primarily to die and rise again. That is the core of Jesus' ministry. We see Him as Prophet, Priest, and King. But His most common title was **RABBI**, or TEACHER. We think briefly of **Jesus as a master teacher**. Dr. Howard Hendricks quotes Dr. Ronald Allen about Jesus' uniqueness.

> ➤ We tend to link a great teacher with a great institution. Jesus had no such ties.
> ➤ We tend to think of a great teacher as one who makes difficult things less complex. Jesus seemed to show new complexities even in simple things.
> ➤ We tend to anticipate that a great teacher helps us face life more independently. Jesus kept insisting that life must be lived in full dependence on another.
> ➤ We tend to associate a great teacher with technical language of his or her field. Jesus used simple language and everyday things.
> ➤ We tend to link a great teacher to his or her brilliant, erudite students. Those who learned best from Jesus were the poor, the lonely, the simple.
> ➤ We tend to think of a great teacher in the setting of a classroom. Jesus' classroom was a hillside overlooking the Sea of Galilee, a corner of a living room, a walk along a path, a small space in a little boat.
> ➤ Today we tend to look for a teacher to use multimedia tools. Jesus' tools were the heavens, the fields, mountains and birds, storms and sheep, a vineyard, a well, and a banquet. In short, whatever was around He would use as a teaching tool.   (Allen, *Lord of Song*, Multnomah Press, 1985, pp. 57-58, cited in Gangel & Hendricks 1988, 15)

We also think of great teachers as writing great books to preserve his teachings. Jesus wrote no words except in the dirt, and His biographers began writing only about 20 years after His death. Still, His teachings are with us today!

The majority of occasions when Jesus taught were initiated by others' questions. Or, like the rabbis, **Jesus taught by inquiry** to make people think: Which?, Why?, When?, How? What is better? Their responses shaped His further teaching to meet the needs that they revealed: ignorance, unbelief, fear, demonic influence.

As a teacher, Jesus lived in the social context of those He taught; drew on familiar items and experiences as object lessons; was always on duty apart from times when He withdrew for the purpose of solitude and prayer; expected His hearers to act on what He taught; confronted those who were improperly comfortable in ritual religion; comforted those who were aware of being unworthy sinners; and became the center of gravity of any group He entered.

Be ready for unexpected teachable moments!

2

WHAT DO WE TEACH?

It is a gross oversimplification to just say, "We teach the Bible!" That is true, of course, but while "Bible" means "book," it really is an encyclopedia. That is a lifetime of teaching material that is useful for spiritual development.

Let's think together about **CURRICULUM**. That is the full range of topics that our church seeks to teach in its training programs for all believers. In our case, we are looking at what ADULTS ought to learn, whether or not they are building on a life-long foundation of Sunday school training.   [More on this later.]

ABF, or **Adult Bible Fellowship**, or whatever names are now used instead of "Sunday school" for adults, is NOT designed to train all laymen for full-time ministry as professional ministers. This is subject matter useful for all adult believers as they seek to grow, and to serve the Lord in their family settings, work environment, neighborhoods, and other normal interaction with fellow-citizens of our town. Candidates for careers in the ministry will study many of the same topics, but at a deeper technical and philosophical level in Bible college or seminary.

When churches use the curricular materials of a publisher of such materials they find a wealth of materials designed by men and women who are professionals in both Bible scholarship and educational principles. When they are produced within the association or denomination of a given church, so much the better since the materials are prepared precisely for a church just like ours. We will keep such teaching materials in mind as useful resources, but also think about how to prepare our own teaching materials.

We look at training for voluntary students of the **Bible**, its **doctrines**, and its directions for living the **Christian life**. That sounds like the OUTLINE for our curriculum! Let's work on that project together. Adult teachers can coordinate with each other and the pastor to avoid overlap and repetition.

TEACHING THE BIBLE

Both teachers and students need both a macro-view and a micro-view of the Bible, the big picture and the details, using both a telescope and a microscope. Each of these topics could be done in a quarter (13 weeks, or 12 due to special days in the church calendar), but not necessarily in this order.

THE BIBLE: AN OVERVIEW:

Bible History: Old Testament beginnings, Creation & flood & scattering to fill the Earth

Bible History: OT patriarchs, formation of Israel as a nation, Law, Kings, split into two kingdoms

Bible History: Old Testament Poets and Prophets

Bible History: New Testament, Life & teachings of Jesus

Bible History: New Testament, Expansion of the Church

Bible letters: Epistles to the NT churches

Revelation: Future Events

How we got the Bible: Process of writing it all down

How we got the Bible: Preservation and Translation

THE BIBLE UP CLOSE:

Studies in individual books of the Bible may well be the

principal items on the menu, our curriculum, through the course of years. Some books merit detailed study for two or more quarters (Genesis, Isaiah, Psalms – in sections, John, Acts, Romans, etc.). Some books can be studied in groups in a more cursory manner (post-exilic history of Israel, Minor Prophets, the Epistles of John, etc.) Dig in!

When we plan meals we seek variety, not just a cycle through five essential dishes. So in our Bible teaching we seek to vary our presentations with a mixture of Bible books, doctrinal topics, and helps for the Christian life. Let's keep that in mind as we survey the range of doctrinal topics that are based on the Bible verses we will include, but are not exposition of any one Bible book. One great advantage of exposition of Bible books is that they bring to our attention the very problem areas that we still need to resolve but tend to miss.

As we select doctrinal topics we may find certain areas that are particularly timely due to events in the world at large or in the Christian world, or even our Association of churches. We follow the traditional divisions of Systematic Theology but tend to stay away from technical terminology or issues of historical interest in the past that hardly touch our present experience. This will not be baby food, but should not be topics that only the few theology nerds will enjoy. This is food for the real life of real Christians in the real world. What does the BIBLE say about doctrinal topics? We suggest some subtopics, but only YOU as teacher will sense what will feed your people a useful spiritual diet, and add as needed. You can also be sensitive to issues that the pastor has addressed in his own schedule of preaching.

Keep in mind that this is for Sunday school, not for seminary. We are not teaching at a level for professional ministry but helping laypersons function adequately within the churches. BTW, "**LAY**" comes from Greek *laos* meaning "people." So nobody is to think, "I'm ONLY a layman" since that is like saying, "I'm only human." The LAYpersons ARE the church, not merely in the church. So we are thinking of training workers within the churches, not over them.

The Doctrinal Topics we list are not each an entire course of study, though many are. Some are deep enough for series; some are individual class lessons. Doctrine means *teaching* and simply organizes Jesus' teachings by topics, together with the rest of the Bible. It is thought through, analyzed, and used as the basis for a philosophical and theological approach to the whole body of truth. But for ABF we do not complicate essential truth with technical terms and contrary arguments. Still, we explain the theological terms used in the Bible so we understand the Book.

Here are some suitable doctrinal topics for study.

DOCTRINAL TOPICS for Class

How do we Know spiritual Truth? -- The inspired Bible
How did inspiration work?, and illumination now?
How did we get our Bibles?
Which is the 'right' Bible version? Is there one?
What is God Like?
What if There Were No God?
Are the other religions valid?
In What Sense is God our Father? Is He Father to all?
How and why do we pray?
What is the Trinity?
Who is Jesus Christ?
Why was His Life so Important?
Why did He teach about the Kingdom more than the Church?

Why was His Death so Important?

Why was His resurrection so Important?

Why was His ascension so important?

How is Jesus our High Priest?

Who is the Holy Spirit?

How and when do we get the Holy Spirit within us?

What does the Holy Spirit DO for and within us?

Does the Holy Spirit make us do exotic things?

Who or what are Angels and Demons?

How do we resist temptation?

What about Wicca and the occult?

What do angels do for us?

What is human nature really like?

What is biblical Psychology all about?

What are *soul* and *spirit*?

What is sin, and what are sins?

What is forgiveness? How?

What are the *old man* and the *new man*?

What does it mean to be "lost" and "saved"?

Who pays for the "free" gift of salvation?

Can a person get saved and then be lost again?

Are we born or adopted into God's Family?

What is the *TULIP* some churches talk about?

Do we choose God, or did God choose us?

What about babies who die?

What about the zillions of people who never heard of Jesus?

Is Jesus Christ really the ONLY Savior?

What is Heaven really like?

What is the "true church?"

Does baptism save our souls?

How do churches function?

What does going to church do for us, anyway?

Why are there so many denominations? Is that good?

Why do we call some churches *cults* when the people are so nice?

What do "Baptists" believe?

Is Jesus really coming back? When and how?

What is this 'Rapture' thing about?
Why is there such a time of 'troubulation' ahead?
Tell me about the Kingdom of Christ!
What comes after the Kingdom of 1000 years?

We could readily have many more – or many less – topics of doctrinal study, depending on what people need to know. Many of these introductory lessons can lead to expanded studies of those **doctrinal topics**. We study the Bible book-by-book and doctrine-by-doctrine to get all God intends for us. Which doctrines are **essential to Christianity**, and which follow **denominational preferences** among some biblical Christians?

One valuable study would be the **Articles of Faith** of our own church. Work through that in more detail than is usual simply because it is the basis of our fellowship in that church. Membership classes skim over this looking for any veto from future members, but little study is afforded at that point. It should come along later for all members of every church, however detailed or simple is the doctrinal statement.

Along with doctrinal topics we can occasionally **explore other religions**, or cults that claim to be Christian. Any such religious movements that are strongly represented in our community would be of greater interest than just studying about religions that rarely touch us.

Religions can be approached by studying the history and the beliefs of each one. Or, we can study select doctrinal topics and then see what other religions believe about them. We moved through several major doctrines to see what the Bible said, and then compared what Islam, Buddhism, and Hinduism had to say about those same topics for comparison.

Our class did a major study on Roman Catholicism and its beliefs and how it is practiced, in a dozen or so key themes. We consulted recent Catholic sources, and used the current Catholic Bible, *The New American Bible*, seeking to understand rather than attack the movement. We compared their teachings with Bible teaching, seeking understanding. A class could do a similar study of the Eastern Orthodox Church or a non-Christian religion if there are many followers nearby.

The major **cults** for concern are Mormonism and Jehovah's Witnesses, but other cults may be hard at work to win over our townspeople, calling for such study. Our town has a coven of witches active in Wicca. What do they believe and practice?

Christian adults ought to know essentials about Islam, Buddhism, and Hinduism. Who wears head scarves? Who wears turbans? Aren't most of them peaceful?

But, wait! There is more. We can make another list of a zillion or so helpful topics on what the Bible teaches about many dimensions of our **Christian lives**, personally and as families. We will suggest a number of them, but will find that the Bible is a virtually inexhaustible fountain of counsel for growth in our real lives. This can include study of the life of some key **person** in the Bible.

THE CHRISTIAN LIFE: AN OVERVIEW

- ➢ What does it mean to love God?
- ➢ What does it mean to fear God?
- ➢ What does it mean to love my neighbor? Or hate him?
- ➢ Who am I now? What does "in Christ" really mean?
- ➢ What are the ways to pray?
- ➢ How does prayer really work? Why? How?
- ➢ What are daily devotions?

➤ What are the basic spiritual disciplines?
➤ How do I 'walk in the Spirit' now?
➤ How do I get rid of these old bad habits?
➤ Is there any real help when I am tempted?
➤ Is gambling OK for Christians?
➤ What are spiritual gifts, and what is mine?
➤ Who gets to serve in the ministry full-time?
➤ How do I help a friend accept Jesus as I did?
➤ How do I help my friend caught in an oddball religion?
➤ How do I get along with unsaved friends and family?
➤ Does God really want my money?
➤ How do I learn what is in the Bible?
➤ Does God care about sex before marriage?
➤ What does the Bible say about marriage?
➤ Is there Philosophy in the Bible?
➤ What is 'justice' in society in a biblical sense?
➤ What happens to people who had an abortion?
➤ What happens to people who commit suicide?
➤ What is spiritual growth, and how is it done?
➤ Why do some saved friends go to other churches?
➤ Are we supposed to talk in weird languages at church?
➤ Do I have to tell the truth about EVERYyhing?

Our local church is our spiritual home. This is where we get our best spiritual meals and share such nourishment with others. We are glad when there are other sound, Bible-believing churches in your town. But we do not help ourselves, or any of the churches, by just hopping around from church to church week after week. No church is THE ideal church.

We do best to find our church home and settle in for the long haul, committed to learn and teach there. Stability and steady growth indicate a healthy church where people are at home. Such membership and attachment allows us to stay and teach, rather than being a perpetual visitor. We can get involved in outreach and inreach ministries, keep in touch with their missionaries around the world, and set a strong standard of faithfulness for our families and those who watch us.

You are a TEACHER. Are there certain areas of this broad curriculum of special interest to you? Once you teach a set of classes to your adult class, it might be welcomed by the Youth Pastor for a briefer version for the young people of the church. You might become a specialist in some areas, with some additional online studies. But your first line of duty is to ingest all that knowledge and counsel into your own life, to live it as a model for others to grow on.

Our toughest question is often, "What do I teach next?" (if we are not using regular published curricular materials). When we are doing our own studies we can ask ourselves, "What do I need most in my own life and walk?" Look over a menu like our lists here for suggestions. One may tickle your fancy.

We should ASK THE CLASS what they would like to study. Keep a list of future topics, doctrines, or Bible books to meet their needs. Sometimes there are other people in the church with expertise in a needed area whom you can invite for a series of lessons: personal evangelism, creation science, managing your money, raising teenagers, promoting missions in the church.

At times your teaching will parallel what the pastor has been preaching. That is not a problem, as long as your comments about his comments are supportive and in agreement. The ABF class is NOT the place to air disagreements with the pastor over microscopic issues. You are one element of his larger teaching ministry, and you share the same objectives.

**The Bible is an inexhaustible supply of wise counsel
for the Christian life and walk.**

We will always remember that ABF is a BIBLE class. Most of our study topics will be part of the Bible, or about the Bible, or how to learn the Bible. And the intended outcome is knowing how to LIVE the Bible. So, there are biblical topics related to our Christian lives, our resources, our struggles. If we only teach Bible facts but not how to live them we eventually teach people that what the Bible says does not really matter.

Even when we use a book with helpful chapters on Christian living, we should look up the Bible verses and discuss their application rather than just wallow in good advice. Encourage class members to READ THE BIBLE: daily, in the book we study and the whole Book. Encourage them to read the ENTIRE Bible in one year, or two or three years if that fits their reading speed better. But remember that when we receive a love letter we read the whole thing and think warmly of the one who wrote it. Read God's entire Word to us!

Since the Holy Spirit is the ultimate Author of the Bible, we will consciously seek His light in our discussions of what the Bible means and how to live it.

CURRICULUM DESIGN

CURRICULUM is equivalent to the menu in a restaurant. It lists all of what the kitchen offers, but often does not serve every meal every day. Customers can select one meal at a time and enjoy variety by their selections. Any school has a similar list of what it offers, but the selection at a given time is much more limited, often depending on what the students need at a given time to get the full range of "meals" that they need for a balanced diet.

When a school, this one or your ABF, plans its "menu" of offerings it begins with an understanding of what is needed to move incoming students to what is designed for outgoing students to be able to do. Compare before and after.

INCOMING STUDENT

> ➤ Entry status: What are their credentials?
> ➤ Entry behavior: What are they able to do in reality?
> ➤ Expected purpose: Going on to grad school?
> ➤ Expected level of function: Laypersons as teachers

The difference with ABF is that it is **open-ended** and the students never 'graduate.' This is life-long learning at its finest. When a church has a training program for its adult and teen teachers it has a similar list for perpetual upgrading of the teachers' knowledge and practices in that vital ministry.

Our open-ended character is both an advantage and disadvantage. We will take ANY person ready to study. We NEVER say, "You've got it all, so stop coming." We are developing life-long learners of God's Words and ways, just like us. We trade off control of our student body definition for a 'y'all come' invitation, creating some uncertainty about the capacity of students. Membership is sort of self-limiting as people are free to choose the class they prefer, normally more by social matching than lesson subject matter.

We as teachers enjoy the liberty to select our own topics for study. But we do well to **PLAN variety into our teaching** so we avoid parking on our own favorite parts of the Bible. We have spoken of **three categories of study topics:** book or biographical studies, doctrinal studies, and Christian life studies. Let's think about a regular **rotation** among these three options so we don't get stuck in a rut of one approach.

My favorite is book studies so we are consciously studying the

Word. That brings us to may doctrinal issues which we can expand as we come to them. It also addresses many topics of the Christian life that we might not otherwise open up for detailed study. On the other hand, doctrinal and lifestyle courses get us into areas of the Bible that may not get much attention in book studies. But I can't just follow my own instincts when I have a roomful of healthy minds. We ask for suggestions and listen to their hearts for direction as to what WE want to study together.

Most of our consideration in our little book is about lesson planning. Publishing houses that prepare teaching materials for ABF have their own curriculum design specialists who consciously plan and balance their curricular offerings on a broader level as well as lesson plans. When we develop our own materials we are responsible for sound planning along with sound theology. Keep in mind that ABF is...

- ➤ **ADULT**: Classes are designed for adults, young and older, who are getting food for their spiritual lives whether new or maturing believers. Adults are expected to think for themselves, take initiative, be aware of their environment, and live by the principles they deem important.
- ➤ **BIBLE**: The essential content of every class is Bible study, not just good advice or pop psychology even as they contribute to the mix. The Bible is applied to real life so it is not a revered book on a shelf, but our guide.
- ➤ **FELLOWSHIP:** The total experience draws people together in a shared environment of hearing and speaking about biblical lifestyle. The awareness of one another enriches what might otherwise be solo study of information. We teach each other.

3

HOW DO WE STUDY THE BIBLE?

EXPLORE THE TEXT.

Exploration is travel through new territory to discover all that is there, both open and hidden. Think of yourself as an explorer bravely scaling new heights, or as a prospector persistently seeking rich deposits. You will peer into valleys and under rocks. Well, ok, you will peer into paragraphs and sentences and words. Like other explorers, you don't know what you'll find – or if you will even like it. You will find yourself in a dead end and have to back out of the box canyon. Well, some rabbit trails are not profitable to follow.

You get the point. We want the unfamiliar to become familiar. The Table of Contents will come to be a map of the region and we will learn to go directly to the right places. Learning the order of the books of the Bible is not just kid stuff. It is like learning the alphabet as essential useful info.

All of this seems to point to Bible book studies. But even with topical or doctrinal studies there are one or more key passages that merit this kind of attention in your study. It is BIBLE study, after all, even as we slice the cake in a different direction.

You will always find more in your study than you can present in class. That is your teacher's bonus. What was exciting for you in your exploration may come across as tedious detail.

CHECK OUT KEY WORDS.

The message of God is expressed in words. Words are the vehicles for carrying God's ideas from His mind to ours and on to our students. With verbal inspiration, each word in the Word is important, whether or not we are equipped to study the text in the original languages. If you can, do so. If not, there are many excellent tools available to help us clarify the meaning of the words used. Go ahead and read some other verses using the key terms, explain how each verse contributes to our understanding of the term, and return to the main text. Always relate the collateral material to the main text so it is clear that you are studying that passage and its central theme or message.

USE AVAILABLE TOOLS

The **CONCORDANCE** is an essential Bible study tool to find where specific words are used elsewhere in Scripture. Bible Gateway is an excellent resource to keep handy on your computer, used to list verses where your key word is used in the whole Bible (in the version you specify) or parts of it.

"Young's for the young, Cruden's for the crude, Strong's for the strong." That is not written in stone. Each has advantages. All of these are based on the King James Version.

Some words in English may express several different words in the original Greek or Hebrew, so if you can find those shades of meaning, and it is germane to the lesson, explain it. Be sure to clarify the meaning in terms of the host language you are using since English is not the original language of the Bible. Some such details you may enjoy yourself as the teacher's bonus, though they do not enter into your presentation of the lesson. Rather than have the class read 10 parallel verses, select the two or three that contribute new dimensions to the topic in the main passage, and wring the meaning from them to benefit the students. Be aware of other helpful resources.

- ➤ The **BIBLE DICTIONARY** offers us useful technical background on how the ancient biblical cultures functioned. Find such books or their online versions.
- ➤ **BIBLE COMMENTARIES** explain words and principles verse by verse, or paragraph by paragraph. We tend to look up the more difficult matters, and find that the commentators ignored them, or gave an answer with no explanation or consideration of alternatives. It is good when they do shed light on difficult passages.
  - o Exegetical commentaries call for seminary training.
  - o Expository commentaries are for any educated users.
  - o Expository sermon series are how pastors preached the messages.
- ➤ **STUDY BIBLES** have occasional explanatory notes within the range of interests of the editor, whether more devotional, or historical, or grammatical. They come with a variety of translations.
- ➤ **TOPICAL BIBLES** collect verses on an array of subjects so you have the full verses in front of you. See such topical Bibles edited by Nave (also online), or Elwell, or MacArthur. The Biblical Encyclopedia section of the Thompson Chain Reference Bible has long been helpful, though in many cases it has only the references.

MESSAGES.

The words form sentences and paragraphs. These are the basic building blocks of our thinking. We latch onto basic concepts and then combine them into larger ideas and plans. Newer translations of the Bible show paragraph breaks, sometimes with headings. Keep your focus on the message of the text. Your exploration should involve the 5 + 1 newspaper reporter's basic questions, useful for analyzing any passage of Scripture, **5 Ws and an H.**

> ➢ **WHO?** Who are the **persons** involved here, including God? What is their history? What are they promoting? Who are they related to, within the story? What is their basic character and nature? Are there men or women or both, and how does it matter? Are the people independent, or under the control of outsiders? How does their character affect what they do or do not do? Which persons influence which persons? Who is friendly with whom, or out of sorts with whom? Are they old or young? Well or sick? Wealthy or struggling?

> ➢ **WHAT?** What is happening? What specific **events** are shaping the flow of the story at hand? What just happened, and what is about to happen? Does the sequence of events contribute any significant lessons? Are there warning messages in the consequences? What objects are important? What value is being exchanged or taken or given? Is there money or land in view there? Is this specific activity part of a larger picture of events which influence it? What is going on there? Be a detective at a crime scene, examining traces.

> ➢ **WHERE?** Describe the general **location** of the action: country, region, city, or town, or rural area. Is there

special meaning associated with that place? Did other important things happen there, with lingering influence? Is the setting of the story important? (in a certain house, by a well, under a shade tree, on a special mountain, near a tape recorder).

➢ **WHEN?** What is the **time frame** of the story in the flow of history, in relation to the rise of key political figures, or in the lifetime of certain key persons? Is another event about to take place? Or has something special just occurred? Is it time for war, or peace, or sunrise, or supper, or sleep?

➢ **WHY?** Why did this happen? Can we imagine what will result from this? Again, is this a single event in isolation, or one link in a chain of events? How is this event more important than other similar ones? Is it for God, or against God and His purposes? How did this event change attitudes, or history, or nothing? Why is this event or person important to us? Can we see why God allowed this to happen, with our hindsight? Was it grace or judgment?

➢ **HOW?** Can we figure out what caused this event or relationship? HOW could this happen? How did it happen? What sequence of events brought about whatever happened? Should it have happened that way? What were the specific processes or steps that made up the overall event? Could some tragedy have been prevented? How should Christians act and react?

You THINK about those answers, but most things you unearth don't get included in your lesson. Not all of them are significant for your lesson, but you prepare to teach by being aware of more than you will teach. Some of those questions may well be raised in discussion, so you have a head start by having faced them already. YOU get enriched, whether or not it is used in this lesson. You have a long future as a teacher, and your own education is life-long.

FOLLOW LINKAGES.

With a concordance you can check where else some **key words** are used in the same book, by the same writer, and in the larger view of the Bible. You will not try to bring every **parallel passage** into this lesson, but you can look for those that shed significant light on the meaning of this word in related verses and arguments. On a larger scale, are the same ideas expressed or illustrated elsewhere in the Bible in somewhat different terms? What other passages does this passage evoke in memory? What does this truth lead on to, or away from?

Most important biblical principles are discussed, or lived out in experiences, in more than one spot in the Bible.

BOIL DOWN THE THEOLOGICAL TRUTHS FOR LIFE.

Theology is not merely a list of statements about God and His workings. Those basic propositions are there, to be sure, but they lead us to ask, "So what?" and take the measure of the consequences. Truth about God roots us in reality and allows us to build firm lives that endure hardship and opposition.

The study of theology leads us to worship our God in new terms and deeper awareness of His person and activities. So, we examine our Bible passage for ideas about God and His working so we can seek to build new God principles into our own lifestyle. A phrase in our text will be part of the larger witness of Scripture about elements of the nature or activity of God, so we can pursue the fuller picture along those lines. Theology drives worship as truth drives us to God Himself.

Theology is "the study of God" and is not to be technical detail remote from life. The meat of Bible study is not just for scholars. God intends His Word for all of us.

EXPAND TEACHING ON DOCTRINES.

As you study a passage, note what it says about any of the major doctrinal themes in the Bible. What does it say about God? Creation? Angels or demons? Mankind? Sin? Jesus Christ? The Holy Spirit? Repentance and saving faith? Election and God's sovereignty? Redemption and regeneration? The church? The return of Christ and end time events?

You will find statements of such importance that it is timely to pause to explore this or that doctrinal topic more fully. For example, each chapter of First Thessalonians ends with some reference to the return of Christ, so at some point in a study of that book it would be appropriate to pull all of those statements together for a doctrinal study of final events, or just the Rapture, and look at key parallel passages as well. "Doctrine" means "teaching." Don't let it be scary.

SEEK THE SPIRITUAL APPLICATIONS AND LIFE LESSONS.

Now we get to the point of our Sunday school lesson. What are we to DO about these principles we've discovered? We cannot afford to begin with mere exhortation to this or that type of behavior. **First** we lay the foundation from the text of biblical truth, and **then** derive motivation from God's heart and mind about the direction of the matter, and **then** encourage one another to live along those lines now seen clearly as the will of God for us.

Biblical principles always drive biblical behavior.

Application is drawn out of the text, not just from common wisdom and backed up by an occasional verse. Proper exhortation is the exposition of Scripture as it impinges on our daily lives. We as the teachers are just as much under the microscope and under the gun as are our students, especially when we teach adults. Lead them to love to study this way!

WARNING: We are not to begin with our application and then just look for verses to support it. Exhortation is based on what the Bible says, so we encourage reading and study of the Bible so the Spirit of God can be the primary exhorter.

We may notice that some topics are left out. "There is variety in the Family of God," and some doctrines do not prevent people from joining your church. Many doctrines matter; some don't define who is, or is not, a Christian.

> **CARDINAL DOCTRINES** define who is a Christian, and, in our case, who is a Baptist Christian. It is all right to be ignorant of details. But if someone opposes key doctrine they are not ready to join this church. They are welcome to attend, but not to vote. For example, if a friend says, "I seek to follow the example of Jesus, but I don't like all that blood stuff, or think the resurrection is a fact," he is not really a Christian in any historical or biblical sense. So cardinal doctrines are of primary importance.

> **SECONDARY DOCTRINES** are not as clearly defined by the Bible, and do not determine whether someone is saved or not. For example, when the Church is 'raptured,' or taken up, will those believers be visible or invisible? There are various opinions, with saved people on both sides of the question. Also, some matters of church administration are seen differently by believers of different denominations. For example, is the church

ruled by the congregation, or by a board of elders? There are good people on both sides. But they gather in different churches so each one is at peace. That is why denominations are helpful. Once we're all in the Kingdom we will all learn, but for now both work, but respectfully separate for the sake of peace.

DENOMINATIONS are accused of dividing the Body of Christ. But the truth is that denominations facilitate the practical unity of the Body of Christ. Just imagine that there was only ONE church in each town, and each was "Christian" in the sense of combining all Evangelical Christians in one congregation. That church would immediately and always face serious questions, even presuming that it stood for Evangelical doctrines.

- ➤ Could its pastor be a woman?
- ➤ How is the congregation governed? By the pastor? By elders? By the full congregation?
- ➤ We all agree that baptism is a Christian rite, but when and how does it take place? Can infants be baptized? Does it matter if such children are from saved or unsaved families?
- ➤ Do they wait until after conversion to be baptized, or earlier in life?
- ➤ Are people to be baptized by immersion? By sprinkling? Does it matter?
- ➤ Are people elect because they converted, or do they convert because they are elect?
- ➤ Can saved people lose their salvation? If lost again, can they be saved again?
- ➤ Can a church cooperate in ministry only with churches with which it agrees fully about everything?
- ➤ Should believers be encouraged to speak in unknown languages in church?

> ➤ Can believers marry only other believers?
> ➤ Can the church marry people of the same sex, or races?
> ➤ What translation of the Bible will be used in public??
> ➤ Will the Rapture of the Church be next?

The list of issues can go on and on. These are some of the doctrines and practices that are distinctive to this or that Evangelical denomination or movement, today, in our country. Some say, "None of this matters. What matters is for all of us to worship and serve together, undivided." The only way that could work is if every member let go of their doctrinal convictions for the sake of 'peace.' That induces internal tension. The tendency today is to minimize denominational distinctives in non-denominational stew.

What is called "brand loyalty" in commercial settings is evaporating in religious settings as people seek churches where they feel good and find friends. The denominations and associations formed out of strong convictions (or ethnic traditions) find that after a couple of generations those convictions do not carry as much weight, and families of immigrants have morphed into the local citizenry. The structures continue, but without the same urgency. Where it is strongly held doctrines that distinguish Christians from one another, the steady teaching maintains their integrity.

It is better to allow those who embrace this or that set of doctrines within the gospel to meet separately, and regard each other with brotherly respect. That is the value of denominationalism as it respects the varieties of interpretive systems and particular traditions. All born-again Christians are Family, but are not identical twins.

4

WHAT IS "ORTHOTOMIC" BIBLE STUDY?

We often refer to **2Timothy 2:15** to encourage study of the Bible. Its familiar words in the KJV are *Study to show thyself approved unto God, a workman that needeth not to be ashamed, rightly dividing the word of truth.* Let's focus on two key words in this wonderful verse.

> ➢ **STUDY** does not mean to "study" as in going to school, hitting the books, and this is reflected in other translations. This verb means "be fast," and indicates our haste, our studiousness, and thus our eagerness, to accomplish something. So we can properly understand the command as, *Make it your highest priority to present yourself to God as an unashamed worker.* That is exactly what we want to do!

> ➢ **RIGHTLY DIVIDING** translates a word used only here in the New Testament, literally meaning **"cut straight."** It could treat plowing a straight furrow, cutting a stone straight to fit into its place in a wall, or cutting along a straight line. This rare verb is in the form of a participle, used as an adjective, so I take the liberty to create the adjective **"orthotomic"** directly from that Greek word.

The real problem is to find what that word means related to Bible study. It clearly indicates following the True Word closely or teaching it quite precisely and accurately, "cutting straight" with it, so "handling it well" or "wielding it as a sharp and powerful weapon" expresses that too. We teach what the Word was intended by its Author to teach!

Nobody has heard of "**orthotomic Bible study**," so we will stick with the familiar term "inductive Bible study."

There are two major approaches to the study of any subject: inductive and deductive study. Both are legitimate and helpful. In our own ABF classes we will take both approaches, but it is good to know when we are doing either one.

> ➤ **INDUCTIVE STUDY** begins by examining the details. We think like a detective processing a crime scene, noting evidence of both major and minor dimensions. "What do we have here?" As the particulars of the investigation are examined, we notice patterns and possible explanations, form a theory, and come out with our conclusions. This will be our major approach to investigating the Bible: from the details to the big picture, notably in verse-by-verse **analysis**. Words matter!

> ➤ **DEDUCTIVE STUDY** begins with the big picture and from it figures out, or deduces, what makes that true within its pieces and parts. In Bible Survey we begin with the inspired Bible as the given entity, and study it as an integrated whole. From there we summarize history, poetry or wisdom literature, and go on to details of prophecy in both the Old and New Testaments. Such surveys are also called **synthesis** which simply means "put together to see it in its entirety."

We also note three overlapping major **phases** of our studies,

➢ **ANALYSIS** is looking carefully to determine "What does the Bible **SAY**?" We began this chapter by clarifying this very question. At our level of study we accept the Bibles presented to us by the scholars who diligently probe the transmission of the text through generations. Variations in text do not affect the Bible's teaching on any doctrine. Revelation is easy to translate but is one of the hardest books to understand. But we readily know what it SAYS.

➢ **INTERPRETATION** is asking, "What does this verse **MEAN**?" We know that a verse says, *Love your neighbor as yourself.* Does that mean that I am supposed to love myself, or that I already love myself (maybe too much) and I owe that same concern to others around me? The science of interpretation is **Hermeneutics**, quite beyond the scope of our study of teaching. Stated principles and rules of interpreting the meaning of text are applied primarily to Scripture, Law, and Literature.

➢ **APPLICATION** is asking, "What am I to **DO** about this truth in the Bible?" Our goal is to lead people (by lesson and example) to incorporate Bible principles into our lifestyle. We are to put into practice what we learn.

In our preparation and presentation of our lessons we will be aware of all three phases of study, and balance them well, not just any one of the three.

WHAT IS INDUCTIVE BIBLE STUDY?

We brushed up against this approach in our previous chapter so it is time to get the details in line for regular use. Again, in inductive Bible study we examine the details to arrive at the big picture and declare its essential principles.

Here are steps in a typical approach to Bible study.

Move through **8 concentric circles** from text to contexts: inside outward in inductive study.

> ➢ Read the TEXT,
> ➢ and then read the larger PASSAGE, sentence, paragraph, [chapter, an artificial added construct, normally good]
> ➢ and on to the entire BOOK.
> ➢ What is the meaning of key WORDS in the text, their grammar, other usage in the Bible and in secular usage?
> ➢ What else did that AUTHOR write along those lines?
> ➢ The WHOLE BIBLE is the best commentary on any single verse of Scripture, read with patience..
> ➢ Events took place in Israeli or Roman, etc. CULTURE,
> ➢ and they were part of the dynamics of WORLD HISTORY.

These steps will vary in their order and depth depending on your prior knowledge of the Bible and history. But this overall approach will help you read the Bible for yourself before consulting commentaries. We do NOT need to explain all the contextual levels in our lessons. But we should be aware of them so we can explore those that are significant to our lesson. Use this as a checklist to be sure you have asked the right questions.

ASK FOR THE AUTHOR'S ENLIGHTENMENT.
This is God's love letter to you! He wants you to understand it. The Holy Spirit is the ultimate Author of the Bible text you are studying and He can instruct you from within your mind when you approach the Bible with reverence and obedience. Remember that its essential teaching may well run counter to what your secular school or neighborhood thinks.

READ THE TEXT.
We'll speak of a verse, but you may well be looking at a chapter

or book of the Bible. Start with a manageable amount, chewing small bites at first. Read it several times in the Bible you normally use. Read it again in other versions you may have within reach, or online. A site like www.BibleGateway.com offers dozens of English versions and many foreign language Bibles for your use. Read the text repeatedly.

WORK WITH AN ENTIRE SENTENCE OR BLOCK OF THOUGHT. Some verses have part of a sentence, or several sentences. Focus on the part you desire to understand in at least one full sentence at a time. It is WORK, so get to love it. Truth is God's gifts wrapped up in words and phrases.

Much of the New Testament is purposely very compact language, especially the epistles. They were intended for detailed study and explanation. Writing materials were expensive so thoughts were compressed. We decompress them.

> ➤ **Ephesians 1:3-11** is all ONE sentence in Greek! It has to be broken up and spread out. It is intended for study in pieces. Rabbi Paul knew how teachers analyzed the text of the Torah for teaching and application.
>
> ➤ Find the core comment: the main verb and object. Then note the descriptors or limitations that qualify and explain that concept. This is the idea of outlining a sentence to analyze its grammatical structure.
>
> ➤ **Nehemiah 8:8** puts Bible reading into 3 distinct stages, or levels.
>
>> ○ **READ THE TEXT.** They read the Law in old Hebrew, a language that many of those in captivity no longer understood well.
>>
>> ○ **CLARIFY THE MEANING.** The reader then translated it into Aramaic, the language they

spoke. It was a mixture of Hebrew and the languages of Babylon (like Yiddish is a similar mixture of Hebrew with German and some Polish, as 'European Hebrew.'). Think of Aramaic as 'Captivity Hebrew.' This might also be like a paraphrase that accurately expresses the meaning of the biblical words in ways that clarify it for new readers. God intends that His Word be understood, not just used as ritual.

o **SPECIFY THE APPLICATION.** What did it mean for their daily lives? This was a focus on the intent of Scripture and how God expected it to be obeyed as a reality.

STATE THE VERSE IN YOUR OWN WORDS.

You can only explain what you understand, so say what this verse says (not what you think about it, yet) in your own way of expressing your ideas. Own it. Embrace it. Say it aloud. This is just what we saw in Nehemiah as the words of Scripture were expressed in words more readily understood by people who were not accustomed to biblical phraseology.

READ THE WHOLE CHAPTER.

As you seek to understand this one verse or key idea, observe how it fits in the rush of ideas within the Bible chapter where it is found. Grasp the context, or the setting of the verse. It is fine to read John 3:16 in isolation, but see it as part of a conversation of Jesus with a smart religious leader who had everything wrong. It is more than a poster at a ballgame. It is fine to read large volumes of Scripture, but for detailed study, stick with a limited passage each time. Be patient and remember that God really wants you to understand it all, in time.

CHAPTER DIVISIONS are a human imposition on the text, as are verse divisions, but with rare exceptions, are well done.

DIAGRAM THE KEY SENTENCE.

Did they teach diagramming sentences in your school? It is not common now, a real loss. This identifies the core idea of the sentence and marks the phrases that modify and explain that key idea. It makes it easier to identify parallel phrases or dependent phrases that support the main idea as subject and action verb. If this is not in your repertoire, skip it. Or learn it.

Example: Romans 8:32 *He shall give us all things.* It is wrapped in qualifying words and phrases.

LOOK UP THE MEANING OF KEY WORDS.

Elsewhere we discussed the main reference works that help in Bible study: concordance, Bible dictionary, explanations of the Greek or Hebrew terms if you have access to such information. It is NOT necessary to study in the original languages to understand the text. What would the meaning have been for original readers? How might we read it differently now?

> ➤ In the ACTS of the Apostles there are at least three different terms translated "**preach.**" Each one focuses on a significant dimension of the process, depending on what Luke wanted to say there. One means "evangelize," giving a beneficial message, without any indication of means by a sermon or a casual conversation. Another is the public address we associate with "preaching" though it does not indicate the nature of the message, favorable or unfavorable. Another word focuses on the authority that underlies a message that is delivered on behalf of the sender. So, when we read "preach" in English it helps to know what term was selected by the

Holy Spirit to convey what was really going on as the gospel was shared on that occasion.

NOTICE THE TENSES OF THE VERBS USED IN THE SENTENCES

This is where study in the original languages is valuable, but there are many excellent reference works that clarify what it says. Verb tenses reflect the nature and timing of the actions involved in the statement, and sometimes the sequence. What comes before or after, and are some actions the cause or result of others? TENSE in Greek is more about aspect of action than of mere timing as past, present or future, etc.

> ➤ We are quite familiar with **Romans 3:23**, *All have sinned and come short of the glory of God.* On a closer look, *All sinned* is in the <u>aorist tense</u> which is not only a simple past tense but summarizes the history of the subject matter. *Come short* seems to be a second verb attached to the earlier auxiliary verb *have* as if it were *have come short.* In reality, *come short* is in the <u>present tense</u> which is not only about now, but indicates continuous action in the present. So we can read the verse, *All sinned and are constantly falling short of [the standard of] the glory of God.* Now we see that it indicates our sins of commission (*all sinned*) and sins of omission (*are falling short*). We have done more than the Law (the expression of God's glorious standard for us) allows but less than the Law demands. That is quite a double-barreled guilty verdict!

WHAT IS THE GENRE, OR TYPE, OF LITERATURE IN USE?

Most of the Bible is simply **historical narrative**. But there are also forms of **poetry** for **praise or lament or liturgy. Wisdom literature** states lessons for all people with its own forms of affirmation or contrast. **Prophetic language** is laden with

figures of speech to represent future reality. **Parables** are a unique form of teaching story. **Epistles** are compact letters for teaching, expected to be expanded and explained and applied. **Apocalyptic** writing was one established genre about end times. So, as we read our target verse we want to be aware of its literary setting so we know whether to expect direct literal meaning or some symbolic representation of truth we dig for. Each type or *genre* of writing has its own rules for understanding its meaning.

> ➢ There are many types of **figures of speech** that are used in the Bible. Our literal approach to Scripture includes allowing figures of speech to be just that. When Jesus spoke of Herod as, *that fox,* He was not calling him an animal but imputing the familiar character of a fox to that man (whatever those people thought of foxes: crafty, wily, or something quite different).

REVIEW THE HISTORICAL SETTING OF THE VERSE.

The historical context reflects the cultures of the various periods. Early Bible historical people had no Bible to read, or lived as the Old Testament was being written through many generations. What was going on in the phases of the history of God's people that sheds light on what was written? Is it in an Old or New Testament setting? What is the social and religious nature of the people involved? Who are the key characters, and what are they like? Remember the principle of **progressive revelation** as the unfolding of biblical truth through the centuries. Don't read the NT back into the OT. We know things that OT people did not.

> ➢ Jewish people rejected the idea that Jesus was their Messiah because they knew prophetic Scriptures that indicated a powerful military Messiah who could free

them from oppression. When a humble teacher offered Himself with an "army" of hillbilly Galileans they could not take Him seriously as the Promised One. Later, they knew from Scripture that anyone who was hanged was cursed by God, so that crucified man could not possibly be Messiah! What they did not know then was that Messiah was to come TWO times, first as the Lamb of God and later as the Lion of Judah. So, when we study OT prophets from our NT perspective we wonder why they could not see what is so obvious. Face it, we would not have understood it then either.

ASK THE REPORTER'S QUESTIONS from the previous chapter.

WHO are the people involved in the story or incident? Who is most influential here? Who else matters here?

WHAT happened to provoke this writing? What does it resolve? What happened? What should happen now?

WHERE did it happen? Is the place significant? Holy? Temporary? Ancient? Owned by someone there?

WHEN did it happen? What just happened? What is about to happen? What slice of history does this event or setting occupy? Is the timing important, or is it for universal practice? What is the time of day? Was it light or dark then? Month?

HOW did this happen? What caused this? What did it cause? What is new or old there?

WHAT DOES THIS SCRIPTURE WRITER SAY ELSEWHERE ABOUT THIS TOPIC?

Several NT writers (Moses, Samuel, Ezra, Paul, John, Luke, Peter) have multiple Bible books that consistently present their inspired message. Did that writer say anything more about this topic? John's epistles explain love seen in his Gospel.

Explore those comments to see if they shed additional light on the passage you are working on. If they do not add information, don't add them to your brief study.

WHAT IS THE PURPOSE OF THIS BOOK OF THE BIBLE?

Your particular passage is part of a larger argument that may, or may not, add light to your lesson. For example, Romans is Paul's major exposition of the <u>sovereignty of God in salvation</u>, but he treats many other related topics in that large epistle. That context may add depth to your own study, but you should not get off on unrelated 'rabbit trails' within one lesson. 1Peter prepares Christians for suffering from political and religious pressures, but not all have that problem. The principles still apply to other types of suffering. When we read Ecclesiastes we need to read the final two verses along with any other part.

WHAT DID YOUR VERSE MEAN TO THE ORIGINAL READERS?

The historical context may clarify why the writer made those specific comments. For example, both Corinth and Ephesus were the sites of major pagan temples of goddesses of love, so immorality was a part of the local religion. In his epistles to those churches Paul was quite explicit about sexual purity and sound marriages because that was part of the instruction they really needed in that grossly sensual environment. Our knowledge of the cultural context clarifies many of the statements made since the various books of the Bible were written to help godly people to please God within the reality of their life settings. We can then extend the principles to fit our current circumstances as they normally apply today.

> ➢ When people heard Jesus say something like, "A certain man had two sons" they knew immediately that He had

made up a story to make a point, what we call a **parable**. It was as if He said, "Once upon a time..." because it was such a familiar literary device for identifying a teaching story. Not all of His parables have that marker, but most do. Some preachers make a big deal out of "a certain man," but the Greek word *tis* is just a particle to indicate "somebody," or John Doe. Of course, Jesus' teaching was in Aramaic, but the Spirit inspired the writing in Greek, so Greek grammar matters. A parable is a story with one point that sticks!

DISTILL THE PRIMARY PRINCIPLE OF YOUR VERSE.

Now that you are deep into the details of your target verse you can identify its key idea. It should coincide with what you are teaching, or add depth and clarity to it. Don't try to make the verse say more than it really says, but don't leave out the essence of what it teaches. This is the core of your lesson.

WHAT DO COMMENTATORS SAY ABOUT THIS VERSE?

We clearly intend to learn as much as we can before we plunge into the comments of noted Bible teachers. There is no good reason to ignore the centuries of Bible studies before we happened on the scene as if our thoughts were so original or profound. We may find that our notions about the verse are way off the track of how godly teachers have presented it, or that we have grasped what the verse truly says. We hope that such affirmation is normal.

A related vital question is, **WHAT IS THE THEOLOGICAL ORIENTATION OF THAT BIBLE COMMENTATOR?** Not all commentaries are written by people who believe the Bible to be the Word of God. Some scholars take great liberties in deciding what the Bible should have said, or otherwise modify the clear meaning toward their works religion. But even among godly Evangelical commentators there are differences of viewpoint depending on their view of Christ's return, for example. It is helpful to know if the commentator is essentially Dispensationalist or Reformed, whether mainstream Evangelical or Pentecostal, whether Premillennial or Amillennial. Their theological orientation will probably color their view of what the verse means for the churches today, just as ours does. We all tend to interpret the Bible within our Bible-based systems of theology.

HOW IS THIS VERSE APPLIED IN YOUR OWN LIFE?
As you weave this verse into your lesson you are thinking of applications in the lives of your students. So, your cogitations must include the impact of the verse on YOUR lifestyle and attitude first. Are you already modeling this principle in your daily practice? Is there something here that is new to you? How would you incorporate this into your walk with the Lord, so you can suggest the same for students? How did you change?

WHAT QUESTIONS STILL REMAIN UNANSWERED?
Identify any gaps in your understanding, and there may be many. Don't hesitate to admit not fully understanding some verses since your students face the same uncertainty. But we do move ahead with what we do know with certainty. Don't wait until you understand it all to begin obeying what is already clear to us! Act on what you know, so you know more.

A good knowledge of the whole Bible is the key to understanding any part of it.

5

HOW DO PEOPLE LEARN?

An Adult Bible Fellowship teacher is to facilitate the learning and application of the Bible, book by book and doctrine by doctrine, by all who are in that class. Educators know that different people learn best by different approaches: hearing, reading, acting out principles in drama, storytelling, etc. This is not simply methodology for teaching, but ways that some people learn effectively.

Teachers tend to presume that others learn best the way they do, or did. If your favorite teacher lectured well, you lecture. Think again. Imagine that you just got your first computer. (Can you remember that far back?) OK, maybe just a new software program you have not worked with yet. You have options:

> Take a class at the computer store and get all the information at one shot (and forget most of it before getting home).
> Read the manual for the big picture. Watch the online tutorials.
> Try it yourself, and look things up when you (finally admit that you) need to get help in parts of it.
> Ask someone who uses that program to come over to

help you   1) get acquainted with its main features, and/or, 2) dig you out when you are stuck.

What is clear by now is that we adults learn differently. And adults learn different kinds of new things in different ways. There is a difference between learning the books of the Bible in order, and learning how to repair and replace something like the carburetor in your (old) car. This calls for different approaches to teaching as well.

Once we grasp that essential concept we can adjust our teaching methods to meet the varied needs of our students. We do not have the luxury of one-on-one tutoring in ABF, but we can vary our methods to reach out to all of them in time.

MAJOR APPROACHES TO EFFECTIVE LEARNING

Educators have long identified several major approaches to effective learning, so we will survey these for ways they can fit into the culture of ABF classes. There are some dimensions we cannot tinker with, but others that we can modify to improve our impact. All the methods do work.

LISTENING TO AN EXPLANATION

Our typical approach to ABF teaching seems to presume that passive listening is actually a means of learning. It is, though it may not be the best for all. We sit and listen to sermons or seminars, live or on television. In a school setting it is enhanced by taking notes, asking questions, and otherwise interacting with the subject matter. But, *Sit & Get Won't Grow Dendrites* (Tate, 2004 title) that is, brain cells. We need to interact.

We need to ask ourselves, "What will help the students to **process** the material several times, instead of just hearing it once?" In ABF we have little structure, and students are not fearful of flunking out since no tests are (normally) given. But all talk and only talk is not a lasting method for learning.

LISTENING AND WRITING

The next step might be to prepare 'Swiss-cheese handouts" on which students write in key words and phrases in the allotted spaces. This calls for a higher level of attentiveness than mere listening, but only if the students are motivated to capture all of that rich teaching. They also have less to carry home. When the handout is a full transcript of the teacher's notes, the students will have all of the intended lesson material in hand whether or not it got fully presented in class. But if that goes unread it still has no lasting value.

Each time the students process the subject matter by needing to express it in their own words, or by thinking about it, they contribute to more permanent learning. It becomes theirs by exercise. So how do we increase that processing?

LISTENING AND ASKING QUESTIONS

The nature of ABF calls for the injection of subject matter material, understanding and applying the Bible. This demands a certain amount of lecture, with or without handouts. But that information can stimulate questions about meaning and the application to life. The teacher will create an atmosphere in the classroom that encourages interaction and questions. Students must know that their queries are not interruptions, but are an expected and welcomed element in the learning process.

The teacher can also prepare and introduce discussion questions that will provoke a variety of other questions as students seek to fill in the gaps in their knowledge. When they contribute insight from their personal experience they are teaching one another by illustrating the life principles that are being discussed. All of that interaction is a healthy stimulation that anchors biblical truth in the minds of all involved. People learn by questioning, and by finding information useful.

HOW DO ADULTS STUDY?

We've thought about how your students learn, but cannot overlook your own need to keep studying and learning. When people have been out of school for a long time they (I should say, "we") forget some of the basic skills for making their learning processes most efficient. This is all the more important when studying on your own as a class of one.

Keep in mind that a teacher does not teach, but encourages learners to learn. Here are some essential **hints for improving learning techniques** for yourself or your students. (Let's face it, very few ABF students do homework, or study up on the passage ahead of class. Nice try! So here are ideas for YOU as the teacher, being a student yourself.)

> ➤ **Highlight** the most important ideas in your books and notes. Books are tools for use rather than artifacts to pass along to the next generation. Underline or highlight key ideas. Scribble in the margins to record your own thoughts or to argue with the author. It is YOUR book, so use it to fit your learning needs.
> ➤ If the textbook is not yours, write key thoughts in your **notebook**. Record those thoughts which are stimulated by your reading since they will soon evaporate. Review them later.
> ➤ As you take notes in class (or in reading alone), score a vertical line to leave a **wide right margin** on each page. Take your notes in the main section to the left of the page, but **write your own thoughts** in that right

column, or outline the major points of the lecture and discussion there. That becomes your Agenda for Action.

➤ When you have **an "aha!" experience** of how class material fits your current work, write it down to capture that useful application. It does little good to remember later that you had a great idea, but can't remember what it was. I am not the only one like that.

➤ **Express your observations** in class. In adult education the students teach one another, so if you have gained useful insight, someone else is dealing with the same problem. This also helps you to reduce that good impression into words as you articulate a concept which is now a part of your active repertoire of skills.

➤ Note **other sources** of information which you find useful. There may be a footnote or the instructor's reference to another book or article or website of real interest to you. Check it out later on to enrich your own knowledge or exposure. Take a look at the Bibliography or Webliography for a given class and look for works which are accessible to you. Check out the most recent works unless your interest is its historical development.

➤ Make it a habit to explore topics of interest on the **Internet**. Whatever you are interested in, a bunch of others have already written up their experiences in blogs or instructional materials or hobby websites. Go looking. Google your topics and go surfing for similar interests by others. Be curious. Stay focused, since there are plenty of interesting distractions. Take an extra step to look up intriguing details. Share the 5% of good stuff you find among the chaff with others in the class. Be careful not to get swept up in the tidal wave of related information. Find the most useful sites and stick with them to avoid endless duplication of basic material. Set time limits to your exploration.

➤ It is helpful to have certain **locations** in your world that are **used only for study.** That may be a certain desk or chair or separate room at home. When you are in that spot you are mentally conditioned to focus on your studies and not on the multitude of other things that clamor for attention. It is time to study now. Set all else aside. Hide that checkbook. Don't play computer games during study time.

➢ As you read the assigned materials, or in class, write down the **questions** that make up the gaps in your own learning. Ask those questions in class when it is appropriate. Others wonder about it too. This can help the teacher fill in what is obvious to him or her but not clear to students. This is a partnership of learning.

➢ **Keep a glossary.** As you encounter new terms of the field in your reading and in class, write those down and form your own glossary of technical terms and jargon used by workers in the field. Mimic the veterans, being careful to distinguish personal quirks from professional behavior and speech. Soon you are talking like a pro. During the rush of class time you can simply circle new terms and then later look them up or define them in your right margin and make an entry in your glossary. Encourage your students to develop this habit.

➢ If appropriate, you can also keep a **list of key dates** and make a timeline to visualize the historical development of your topic (if it fits on a timeline, as many topics do not). Note **key names** of significant persons in timeline.

➢ If your subject matter comes to mind in the form of a chart, or **diagram**, or model, write it down quickly. Later on, you can think it through as a helpful summary of the material. The teacher may even welcome it for future use with other students, or with these. Many people are visual learners, so the relationships of concepts, or the order of events in a process, stick in the mind as a picture or chart rather than an outline or bullet list.

➢ If you are using a computer in class, or after class, you **summarize and organize** the instructional material in ways that are useful to you. Your glossary is readily kept in alfa order as it grows. You can separate out the specific ideas that apply to your work, whether or not they will be on the test. All this is excellent review and reinforcement. Clarify your questions that still need answers.

➢ As you **review** for a test, go for the highlighted parts of the text and handouts. Think through your notes in the right column of your classnotes. Reread your own glossary to get those new terms nailed down correctly.

➢ **Talk aloud** about the topics you are reviewing for a test. Such "private speech" helps to set the concepts in your mind because you framed them in words. Or, explain some key concepts to a friend who can follow in the textbook or notebook to bug you with more questions. Study with a friend and teach each other.

➢ Many find it helpful to set **a schedule for review** times. Hours of intensive writing, or reviewing, bring on mental fatigue. Schedule a 5-minute **break** after 45 minutes of concentration. Go for a walk. Go hug your kids. Reward yourself with a snack. Then get back to work for another 45 minutes. Specify time for study so you do not feel guilty about taking time away from other demands. This IS a part of your ministry, and study merits this portion of your total day. Plan it in practically, and stick to it. Support one another in your study times.

LEARNING is a process that we all have worked at since our first day on Earth. Now that we are teaching, or encouraging others as they learn, we can make that process more effective. Adam and Eve were NOT created with minds full of encyclopedic knowledge. They were equipped to observe, ponder, compare, distinguish, discern, link, theorize, reject bad ideas, and define a matter. They were equipped to form a mental library, BUT all of the shelves started empty. Only humans are made in the image of God which includes rationality, creativity, and the ability to generalize from specific experiences to rules for the future. We CAN learn. Try it!

WHAT ARE THE 5 NORMAL LEVELS OF LEARNING?

We don't just "learn" facts, but interact with them on at least five distinct levels, with increasing difficulty. Our instructional planning should take into account the level of learning which the teacher intends for the student to accomplish. Let's face it, we don't really expect everyone to master every single fact we discuss. If we gave final exams in ABF we would have to factor in our expected level of learning for each item in our teaching.

As we think about "What does it mean to LEARN??" we begin with the five commonly recognized **LEVELS OF LEARNING.** Experts vary, but we offer a simplistic version.

A. EXPOSURE

Students become **aware** of certain areas of knowledge, and are not responsible to do more than have seen it. Such material is not included in tests or projects. Even Albert Einstein reportedly said, "90% of education is learning where to look it up." These TRUSTpages Series books give you Bibliographies, but we don't expect you to recite the bibliographies back to us. You have seen them and know they are there for when you need them. The specific technical facts have a larger conceptual context in which they make sense. We may teach the facts and simply make people aware of the intellectual environment in which they function. Get the facts more than the theories. The teacher's goal for exposure is that when the student encounters this concept later on he can think, "I remember seeing that before" and not be caught off guard. It is enrichment with background material.

B. RECALL

When presented a fact, the student not only can remember having seen it before, but can distinguish it from other similar items, even if she might not have been able to express the idea herself. Recall is best tested in multiple choice questions where the correct response is **RECOGNIZED** among several viable wrong choices. Students should recognize and discern correct information at this level. The danger in multiple choice testing is that students may identify deeply with one of the incorrect responses. Matching tests provide the terms for which the students are to demonstrate they comprehend the meanings. We always have a larger vocabulary in our reading than in our writing since we can recognize words we know but seldom use ourselves. That is recall.

Adults have internal shelves of information which is not always readily accessible. Training helps them to organize those resources and keep them useful. When we read books about things we have already studied we refresh those memory banks, prioritize better, and add a bit here and there, and the recall process is enhanced. It is not memorization.

C. MEMORIZATION

Students can "learn" to recite back, orally or in writing, the information presented with exactitude and confidence. **Rote learning should not be disparaged** as true learning since that memorized material is carried around for later interaction. Still, correct recitation of the material taught does not necessarily indicate that the student has comprehended or absorbed the concepts.

African gray parrots can memorize and recite, even correctly when prompted. But they do not comprehend the meaning of what they are saying beyond some associations that elicit certain responses to certain cues in the environment.

Some things are only "learned" in order. When we are asked

what book follows Jonah we generally have to get a running start with Hosea and recite all twelve of the Minor Prophets in order to land on Micah as the correct response. Some Brazilian students readily memorized the names of their 22 states (back when we lived there) in a set order, but many could not then find many of those states on a map, a quite different skill set. Still, they did "know their states."

In preliterate societies, great value is placed on memorization. People are careful to be accurate and complete since there is an aura of sacredness about cultural lore and family history. The Brothers Grimm traveled far and wide in central Europe to gather fairy tales to write them down, and often found them recited exactly the same in far distant places.

> ➤ One of our colleagues in Brazil worked interior (that is, away from the city) where many people could not read. He distributed tape players with cassettes of common Bible verses which people hungrily memorized so they could recite Bible verses in church services along with those who could read. He had Galatians recorded on tape and people would listen repeatedly until they could accurately recite all six chapters. Illiterate people are not stupid, simply uneducated in written works.

> ➤ One game played at teen camp was reciting memory verses without repeating one already quoted by someone else. One such contest I saw went on for two and a half hours of quoting memory verses until the final teen was disqualified. And we complain that we can't memorize! Since we can read or ask Siri we fail to develop that corner of our own intelligence.

D. EXPLANATION

Being able to express concepts in one's own words demands a

high level of understanding and integration of them into one's repertoire of ideas-on-hand. This is a higher level of learning than mere memorization, contrary to the opinion of some educators who set the precision of memorization above the informality of explanation. It is possible to bluff and fluff on essay questions, but teachers generally know when the student doesn't really understand the matter. Mastery of the information is indicated by one's explanation and application of it in one's own words. A student can recite what is memorized, but cannot explain what is not understood. If we as teachers expect students to express ideas in their own words, we are expecting more of them than mere recitation.

E. PROBLEM SOLVING

Being able to use facts and concepts in the resolution of life problems is the highest level of learning. The information and skills introduced into the memory banks of the learner become resources for creative application in a real-life or lifelike situation. Think of a depressed or tempted student turning to the Bible for verses of encouragement and victory. It works!

Learners can generalize from the lists of principles and processes learned to the application of those in creative ways that solve real problems in life. That includes being able to try different approaches to using the essential principles they learned. They have become embedded in the students as resources for varied lifestyles. Students find they can creatively use the new information to solve real problems they face. Such profound change in a person is properly called "learning." Seek the JOY of learning with them.

SUMMARY: The 5 levels of learning we discussed are: exposure, recall, memorization, explanation, and application to problem solving.

Now that we have identified the levels of learning, we could design a final exam for each series of studies. In designing instruction, teachers can decide at what level of learning each item is to be learned. There are different types of questions that are appropriate for each level. How thoroughly do we expect our students to master the material we so busily give them week after week?

Think about it, even though we do not (normally) have a final exam in ABF. Would that be a good idea? How might it work?

WHAT DOES IT MEAN TO "LEARN?"

We spoke about the nature of teaching as engaging the students in the process of learning. Now we consider the other side of the coin and wonder just what the matter of LEARNING is really all about. After all, that is why we teach!

What do YOU think learning is? What will it take for you to feel like you have "learned" the material in this course? Not all of the information is retained at the highest of the five levels we considered, since some of it is knowing where to look it up when needed.

Here are some basic notions that can lead to a definition.

> - **The student will understand, or grasp, the meaning and utility of the facts and principles that are new.** A light turns on. Pieces of the puzzle get connected to add up to the big picture. Some parts help other parts to make sense at long last. Sometimes a student will grasp the theoretical basis of things that he/she has already practiced for a long time.
>   - My wife Doris taught Music Theory in our seminary in Brazil. One student was a natural

musician, quite accomplished on both accordion and guitar. But he skillfully played in terms of finger positions. As Doris explained chord structure the student was constantly muttering, **"O-h-h, now I get it!"** His good practice was affirmed by new understanding of the theoretical basis of it all. Today he is the highly skilled maestro of the official chorale of their state in Brazil, touring Europe as well as Brazil.

➢ **The student will incorporate the facts and principles into his/her lifestyle** in the ways that connect with the subject matter. True learning is far more than an emotional response of "Wow, that's cool" or similar passing appreciation. When one learns something new the reaction is, "I can put that into practice and adapt it all into my 'normal' way of acting." Many things in a class are already part of students' practice, but a few new ideas will be embraced as part of one's teaching practice. This is our aim in ABF!

➢ **There are some permanent changes in the repertoire of behaviors of the student** as a result of the class. There is a natural deterioration of memory of the material as time passes, and other course materials crowd in on the processing of what is valued as new and useful. Part of the permanent CHANGE is stuff we now know and remember, even if it does not call for new behavior. You can go on Jeopardy and recall facts or trivia that are lodged in your brain. We want to know the BIBLE so we can pull up verses we need, or remember what 2Thessalonians is about, or where to find David's life and reign. During classes we can see the value of asking more questions and doing less lecturing, but we have learned to **adapt** to a new style of teaching when we regularly raise questions and expect students to answer and even debate their answers.

> **Students have really learned a subject when they can teach it.** They put the material together (synthesize it) with their own spin on it, and fully own the facts and principles as their own. Knowledge has flowed from their notebook into their mind and lifestyle. After a while it is just stuff they know, rather than stuff they just heard in class. Their further learning and practice bring insight from other teachers (in person or from media) so they grow to no longer associate their expertise with you, their original teacher of that material. Then we have succeeded as teachers!

MODES OF LEARNING

We have mentioned some different ways that people learn, so let's focus on those and how we can use those channels to teach the Bible.

AUDITORY LEARNING: Some people learn best by listening.

> Lectures, live or recorded, radio, CDs
> Scripture set to music, familiar recorded hymns
> Student reports from buzz groups
> Discussions in group study or full class
> Storytelling: found or composed
> Jokes and humor related to subject matter
> Counseling, coaching, mentoring

VISUAL LEARNING: Learn by observing, watching, reading

> "Graphic organizers" or "mind maps," charts, graphs
> Photos, videos, TV programs, computer-based graphics
> Tutorials, recorded or ...

➤ Live demonstrations
➤ Information set to music, rap, chanting
➤ Daydreaming: thinking of yourself as a contented, competent teacher enjoying ease and success in class: a target to shoot for. Picture your success!

TACTILE, OR KINESTHETIC, LEARNING: Learn by moving, handling materials, touching, building

➤ Guided experience (changing spark plugs or diapers, preparing a lesson, etc.). Watch and then do the same.
➤ Assembling models representing concepts and history
➤ Writing: connecting the mind to the hands
➤ Drawing: relating principles to each other graphically
➤ Acting out events: Passover, drama, producing short video programs, readers act out conversations in the Bible like Jesus' argument with Pharisees in John 5.
➤ Handling samples of biblical building materials, plants

Review this list as you are preparing your weekly lessons. What new approaches will allow students to process your information from the Bible a tad more thoroughly? How can we appropriate several of their learning preferences to get our messages across to them?

Again, we do not simply teach. We stimulate students to learn. The more they are engaged in active learning processes, the more we facilitate their long-term learning. The onus is on them.

6

HOW DO WE PREPARE OUR LESSONS?

Sunday school teachers have two main options regarding the actual material they can teach. Both are potentially fine: use printed curricular materials designed for a class just like yours, or you prepare your own lessons.

We will lay out some procedures for the self-researching teacher, but first we should survey the types of materials available for teachers.

> **DENOMINATIONAL CURRICULUM.** For most churches that are in an association of churches or a denomination, the leaders of that organization prepare curriculum for all ages. Non-denominational churches also have access to those same materials, and to curricular materials prepared by non-denominational presses. Such materials normally have high quality quarterlies for both teachers and students, supported by study questions, visual presentation materials, handouts, and plenty of instructions and helps. Our churches are well served by such a wealth of teaching materials based on excellent teaching by pastors and scholars, then edited by andragogical professionals. To rely on such materials is an excellent choice.

> ➤ **BOOKS BY NOTED AUTHORS.** Teachers can select fine books dealing with topics for the Christian life, books of the Bible, doctrinal subjects, family issues, and a host of other valuable materials for study. Students read the assigned chapter each week and then talk through it in class. Many such books have study guides for just that purpose. These can also be alternated with normal curriculum from time to time, or when certain topics deal with current needs and public issues.

> ➤ **VIDEO SERIES.** There are DVD-based studies by well-known teachers that bring the best of the best right into your classroom. They are not made for student interaction during play unless they are programmed with stop-and-discuss periods. Or a 30-minute DVD can be followed by a 15-minute discussion of issues raised by that teacher or by you, or in a discussion guide that accompanies the digital media.

Our American churches are rich with such resources so the teacher's plea is not, "What can I use?" but "Which shall I choose?" Still, there are teachers [like yours truly] who still prefer to research and plan and write and edit their own lessons. This very TRUSTpages Series of adult study resources is some of the fruit of decades of such teaching. I admit to the advantages of seminary and other degrees, and a career as a Bible college teacher on the mission field and occasional seminary teaching in the decades that followed.

Many others with less outside help just love to study and teach, so they pay the price week after week of studying, analyzing, sorting and writing. Come on along with me on a ride through the maze of lesson preparation for a series of studies in a given topic, book of the Bible, doctrinal subject, etc. Our Heritage Class does not follow a schedule of quarter years for lessons.

HOW DO I PREPARE A SERIES OF LESSONS?

A big step is to DEFINE THE TOPIC for a given quarter, or year, or indeterminate period. "What do we study now?" is a vitally important question. When we are following published curriculum, this question is settled for us, but when we write our own we are on our own here. Normally for adult classes this will be a **Bible book study**, a **doctrinal study** (including Baptist Distinctives), a **biographical study** of a major Bible character, or some dimension of the **Christian life.** Whether a book study or other topic, there should be one main Bible text in each lesson with other verses brought in for support. Call it whatever you will, this is BIBLE school, so the study is always Bible-based. How do we do that well?

1. **DIG INTO THE TEXT.** The best starting point for the teacher is reading the main text over and over. This means repeated reading of a whole book of the Bible when that is the case, or of the passage in view for a given week once into the study. Read several times, in several versions, and even in several languages where you are capable of that. Wallow in the message as if it had been written to you. (It WAS!).

2. **OPEN YOUR HEART TO GOD AS YOU READ** so you measure your own appropriation, application, and obedience to it. Pray through it. Own it. Embrace it. Memorize key verses. Try living out new parts of it. This kind of deep personal interaction with the text is the first step in mastering it and letting it master you.

You cannot teach what you have not learned, and the more you notice and learn on your own the more you have to share with others. The whole point of your class is to encourage others to interact with the text, the Word of God, just as you do. They will not often go into it more deeply or more warmly or more obediently than you do as their mentor. Get a grip on the text and let it grip you. Worship the Lord in terms of what you are learning in your lesson preparation so others can discover similar uplifting truth. It is about the Lord, after all, not about us. We find problems that are treated, so be sensitive to similar problems we experience today. But first, read to learn. Get into this meditation before putting down the first word on paper (or in a computer file).

3. **SORT IT INTO LESSON-SIZED PIECES.** There will be natural breaks in the message of the text. These do not always follow the chapter breaks, though those are natural dividers. Some passages call for careful verse-by-verse and phrase-by-phrase analysis, and others in chapter chunks. Some key words call for special attention, and a side study into where that word is used elsewhere in the Bible.

Look for related enriching principles in those verses rather than just reading and noting that the same word is used elsewhere. What does that verse and context add to our understanding of the key word under the microscope? Some historical or prophetic passages can be reviewed several chapters at a time. You will have a feel for what is appropriate.

There are also natural limits to the comprehension of your students. You may spend hours of joyful study of tiny details, but still need to cram your sharing of the text into the allotted hour – or however much less than that is proportioned to you each week. Instead of rushing through too much material in the limited time, you may expand the number of lessons.

And you will recognize that you will learn a lot that will never make it into your lessons in class. There are historical tidbits, parallel passages, and more that are too much. That is personal enrichment, so just treasure bites yourself, as a chef's treat. Some of it will come up in discussions when the Q&A gets beyond the limits of the printed page or scheduled lesson.

4. **PLAN THE GENERAL TRACK OF THE FULL COURSE OF LESSONS.** You may need to explore a book in 26 weeks instead of 13 or less. Before you begin the first lesson, chart out **how many lessons** will be needed to appropriately cover this book, or doctrine or topic (remembering whatever special days will come along on the **church calendar** during that period). That may change, but at least you begin preparing with a target of 13 lessons, or 26 or 40.

Find out whether you are expected to follow a **quarterly schedule** with other classes, or have liberty to study each topic for as long as it (reasonably) takes to complete it.

Make a rough schedule of classes. Some of that will change later, but start with a workable plan that fits your realities. See if there is some natural transition point to the next lesson series (end of year, start of the school year, etc.) and plan toward that conclusion. If there are **seasonal breaks** (a Christmas or Easter lesson or series, or special national patriotic days that merit Bible study on their roots, Mother's Day, or whatever is celebrated) plan those into your calendar for this course. Try to start a new course at a time when many of our students are not away on vacation.

HOW DO I PLAN EACH LESSON?

We progress from the overall curriculum, to the particular series of lessons, and now to each lesson. We have 45 minutes (or whatever time you have) so how will we use those precious minutes? PLAN the lesson, and stay flexible.

5. **IDENTIFY THE CORE MESSAGE OF EACH PASSAGE.** The point is not to "cover Romans 8 in 50 minutes" but to explore and apply the message of Romans 8 to each person in class. A rich chapter like that needs to be spread out into its constituent topics, normally found in blocks of text. Treat each passage, or major topic, separately as your time frame allows. Sunday school should be far more flexible than regular school, especially for adults. It is more life-related and less schedule-driven by its very nature.

For each chunk of text **identify the message** that shapes that passage. Find the **key verse** if there is one that summarizes the passage. Memorize it. There will be collateral messages, and several layers of applications, but begin with what the text **says** about its key concepts, and then move to selected rabbit trails. Take key points of your outline from the text, even with contemporary titles. You may need to ignore some of the side messages in order to focus on the main message. Plan additional lessons to focus on important side messages. Don't be afraid to simply bypass some sections of Bible text when they deal with minor issues already resolved.

Think about theology! Don't get too technical, but relate the text to underlying truth that is linked to foundational concepts. Does the Trinity show up? Is there some hint about the future Kingdom of Christ? Is there some object lesson about salvation or a character quality in our new life in Christ? When we urge people to live in godly ways related to the lesson, state the biblical/theological basis for that emphasis. It is not just the teacher talking, but God defining behavior.

Read it again. Talk your way through the flow of the thoughts of the text. **Grasp the core message**, and don't miss it in your teaching. That is what <u>God</u> intended to say to His people. Finding that core message may mean you will leave out some other good matters there of lesser importance.

Does a picture come to mind? Is there some **graphic diagram** that charts the relationship between key ideas, or a process that has tangible stages? If you do illustrate your lesson with some graphics, do more than just make fancy lists. Let that diagram do the work of explaining how key concepts interact. And go ahead to explain it in words as well. Use the eye gate as well as the ear gate to get the message into the minds of students.

We talk about "us" not just "you" in applications. When the teacher is a **fellow learner** the students tend to feel at ease to learn and grow too. We maintain a healthy balance between exhortation and the principles of Scripture which are foundational to such a walk. This is not the place for either zeal without knowledge, or knowledge without zeal.

Formulate **questions to help review** the teaching material. Since we don't (normally) give exams we can use the questions as a form of review. We don't have to wait until the end to give a final exam, but can review the material as we go along, or in the next lesson. Tie the lessons together with reminders of the context and purpose of the book or doctrine under study. We can go over the big picture of that book of the Bible, or that area of doctrine, or facet of the Christian life. Repetition is part of teaching, and repeating answers is part of learning. Every time and way that students process the information they are planting it more deeply in mind and heart.

Clearly, we prepare for the short term and for the long term.

A. **GET PEOPLE TO DIG IN TO STUDY AND PARTICIPATE.** The real joy of teaching is seeing our students become learners on their own initiative, and teachers in their own time. We don't just give the answers, but give the tools for Bible study, along with motivation to keep it up, keep it deep, keep it interesting, keep it personal. Let people know what is coming next week and give reading assignments or memory verses in the Bible text. Not many will read ahead, but some will be rewarded.

B. **TRAIN A SUBSTITUTE TEACHER.** Through this entire process you should have someone whom you are mentoring in the preparation and delivery of Sunday school lessons. You will find ways to put him/her to work unless he or she has a regular post in a different class and is your backup when you are not available or for occasional classes. ABF teachers can take a furlough from their mission of teaching.

Work with your co-teacher in the planning, study, and carrying out of the plan for your class. You are not just teaching the Bible, but are training Bible teachers. Look forward to the day when you will step away from that Bible class, leaving it in the capable hands of one you have trained. You may well serve some time as his/her co-teacher, filling in occasionally, working alongside and mentoring gently, providing some resources.

Or he/she may move over to teach another class while you stay put. Either way, you will have contributed to another teacher of the Word of God. Turn them loose!

C. **KEEP THE CLASS A JOYFUL EXPERIENCE.** From our own school days we remember favorite teachers and those we dreaded. Which would you prefer for your students? Once our prepared lessons are uncorked in class they become an experience, not merely a blob of subject matter. Discussion gets people engaged as they share ideas and insights that the teacher never anticipated. The Holy Spirit enlightens people as we teach and learn, enriching the class experience with depth that can never get onto paper. HE is the real teacher, but uses our thorough preparation to honor the Savior we serve.

It is a source of joy, not just to dig out truth, but to open people's eyes to what they can find and enjoy and obey in the Word of God for themselves. The real satisfaction comes when our students become teachers because they have learned to love to study and teach the Word of God. Our success goal is the success of our successors!

We want to sleep peacefully on Saturday night rather than find ourselves in a frantic last-minute search for some elusive idea. When we are duly prepared we rest well.

NOW comes the real test of our preparation: Is my lesson really ready to be used in class? How will I know? A **checklist** allows us to pass judgment on our own work before others can do so. Think about how the lesson impacts your own life, and face whatever changes are needed in your own Christian life.

Follow on...

IS MY LESSON READY FOR USE??

As we prepare each lesson for class we need to inspect our work carefully to be sure it is finally ready to use. This is really needed when we prepare handouts where everyone can see our errors. A checklist helps that final review before we hit the 'print' button on the copy machine at the church office.

- o Scripture passage clearly indicated
- o Treatment of the key principle in the passage
- o Proofreading for correct spelling and references
- o Illustrative material to help explain key terms
- o Review so I know the lesson well.
- o Simple explanation of any complicated verses
- o Several discussion questions planned
- o A bit of humor or human interest
- o Connections to current news or church events
- o REVIEW so I know the lesson well.
- o How-to comments about usable elements of the lesson in daily life
- o Pray through the lesson for what I need to fix.
- o Other applications to home or work life, friends, finances, parenting, temptation, etc.
- o REVIEW so I know the lesson well.
- o Read the Scripture passage in 2 other versions.
- o Is my handout ready for printing and copying?
- o Print a few, recheck spelling and appearance.
- o REVIEW so I know the lesson well!
- o Make copies in church office for handouts.

Whew!

7

HOW DO WE TEACH?

We have the proper ingredients for a class: The Book, a room, curriculum, a teacher, and some students. That is NOT the entire recipe. A good recipe always includes the process of mixing the ingredients in the proper proportions and order and at the proper time. We who are cooks include the spices that make a stew delicious.

So what is the recipe for a delicious adult class? How can we teach the content we want to get across in such a way that the students look forward to coming week after week? Let's think about some ideas for class. We won't do all of them every week any more that we would use all of our spices in every dish. Variety is the spice of adult classes. I have a lot to learn in my own teaching of adults, even after many years of experience, (as I have a lot to learn about cooking after years of eating).

We have surveyed a variety of ways that different people tend to learn more effectively. Now we can look at the other side of that learning/teaching coin to survey methods we can use that complement the varied approaches to learning. Each class will have people all across the range of preferred learning forms, so we will vary our teaching approaches to click with all of them more of the time.

OUTLINE THE LESSON PLAN

For school teachers, this one-page outline is the menu they can follow for teaching each major subject each day. The first time through it is busywork. BUT when you get into class feeling harried and rushed it is the map that guides you through the traffic jams. When a teacher needs a substitute on short notice it is a life saver for one coming in on the middle of a process. Make your own template. **So, what does a LESSON PLAN include?**

1. **The OBJECTIVE or MAIN TOPIC** for this class hour. What do you expect to accomplish in this hour of class? Reduce the lesson to one sentence and tape that in front of you in your study space.

2. **REVIEW** of recent lessons to maintain the big picture. A quiz over that?

3. **MAJOR POINTS IN THE CONTENT OF THE LESSON.** 3? 4?, 5 major points? Not 22. Some of the optional activities will fit different main points in your lesson. Look for variety, and for several ways for students to process your main principles.

    a. Reference to the textbook (in our case, the Bible), maps, historical background

    b. Other helpful resources, examples, stories, experiences, quotes from books or preachers

    c. Visual aids to clarify the principles and their utility

    d. Short (3 to 5-minute) presentation assignments by some students

    e. Discussion questions to provoke thought and application

    f. Exercises to help students process information:

game, drill, video...

4. **SUMMARY** of the key principles in the lesson. Will TESTING be part of your review (ha ha)?

5. **PREVIEW** of the next lesson, for continuity and connection.

Clearly, we prepare for the short term and for the long term. We have been dealing with teaching adults and youth, and will next look at children. After a while, you as an ABF teacher will do most of this by intuition more than in writing. But the exercise is an excellent way to develop proper habits in your preparation for each class. Once our preparation is complete,

HOW DO WE TEACH OUR LESSON?

LECTURE, WITH OR WITHOUT HANDOUTS

The old standby method is to teach the lesson as students follow in their Sunday school quarterlies which, as often or not, they neglected to read and fill in the blanks. People readily accept traditional methods, whether or not they are effective, because, "That is how we have always done it."

Frankly, lecture is still the standard method for getting a mass of subject matter across from teacher to students. The question is whether it is penetrating the minds and hearts of those students. Are they actively learning, or are they passively just waiting for class to end? We do not dismiss lecture since it is so much a standard part of how people get ideas across to other people. They talk about it. They lecture, or preach, even on the radio and on television (though TV enriches the teaching with the video element).

Where we can improve the lecture method is in enhancing the interaction of the people involved, for improved processing of the subject matter by the students. We can improve our personal expression, language, descriptive powers, movement, variation of voice. We can tastefully inject humor, illustrations, and some charts, pictures, stick figures, PowerPoint ®, etc.

LECTURE WITH DISCUSSION QUESTIONS

A good teacher will interrupt his or her flow of content to ask questions that test (oops, did I use the T word?) the students' comprehension of what is being taught? We don't give written tests, but can do some in-flight checking of progress.

Occasional questions can provoke students to rethink what has just gone out to them for comprehension and memory. When they can restate teaching material in their own words it shows a higher level of mastery than just reading back a paragraph from the handout or quoting a Bible verse. We can only explain what we understand. The more outspoken students tend to answer general questions, but the others are processing the information to formulate a response, even if someone speaks out before them. If this sort of questioning becomes a familiar pattern the class could shift to raising hands to volunteer a response, so the teacher can call on the quieter ones, but that is more like school and may not go over well.

Think carefully about questions to ask in class, and expect answers. Adults and teens have ideas and are often eager to share them with others. A key concept in adult education in America is the sense of equality. Each one has something to offer and the right to express one's ideas. Factor that in rather than fight it.

> ➢ Not all cultures presume that students can contribute. When I taught a week in a university in HaNoi I kept asking if students had any questions. Silence. After a few

days of this, a couple of students worked at researching questions from the footnotes of old textbooks just to satisfy my request. They quickly realized they were embarrassing me with technical questions I could not really answer. I had to accept that their concept of a "professor" was that he/she was the fountain of information. To question a professor would be disrespectful, so they had remained silent. Their classroom protocol dictated that they would stand in silence when the professor entered the room until given permission to sit. I had to learn how to be a teacher in Vietnam! Then it all went more smoothly.

DISCOVERY LEARNING

As we prepare our lessons there are certain basic thoughts that come to mind. We have all attended (or taught) classes that are good, but entirely about things we already knew. Often we do well to skip saying those known things to say what comes as a result of those more obvious things. Think beyond the surface. You are responsible to stir up more than the obvious. Link what they know to what more they should know.

Ask questions that allow students to contribute such thoughts. That allows them the satisfaction of contributing, and stimulates their minds to arrive at conclusions they might not have thought about directly. Let them discover what they already know. It is a valuable form of review.

It may feel good to explain A + B + C = D as we complete the logical train of thought. **But in discovery learning** we provide A and B as seminal ideas. We can then ask a question that leads on to fact C and allows the students to conclude Principle D. They get that "aha!" moment that is the joy of learning. And, of course, that works back to us when our students come to a conclusion that we had not thought of, and we get our own "aha!" moment. It is a good thing when the teacher learns from the students.

> If you are teaching someone how to put together a jigsaw puzzle you will first 1) explain the purpose and show the picture on the box, 2) give them all of the pieces, and 3) discuss ideas to get them started on basic procedures like turning over all the pieces and sorting them into visually similar bunches, and finding the edge pieces, then, 4) step back and let them work on the puzzle. They must find their own way through the processes. Their struggle is the real teacher, and they will enjoy that first experience far more than if you just put the puzzle together for them. They are discovering their way, and will do much better the next time around.

The DANGER found in discovery learning is expecting too much too soon, especially if students lack information or notions of process. Input just as little as necessary to motivate and affirm their finding their own way, their own conclusions – with a nudge toward truth, correctness, utility, or whatever level is appropriate with the goals of instruction. It is not true that "whatever you agree on is correct." They still have to stick with the solid facts and come to worthy conclusions.

HANDS-ON LESSONS

We know that children learn by doing. For a children's class on Joshua a teacher might have them build a city wall around Jericho and then march around blowing trumpets. Someone could push the walls outward to fall down. That is fine for a children's class, but it is really just teaching the essential facts of the case. In adult classes we are dealing with more abstract principles of obedience and trust that call for more than some symbolic re-enactment.

Instead we could divide into groups to discuss for a few minutes and then tell the class in turn how the people reacted within the city as they watched the circling army, and then how the troops responded as they marched silently around the city amid insults, and another group describe Joshua's shift from feeling ridiculous to confident to impatient to exultant in this first major trial of his leadership of the nation. Then the full class can analyze all of the spiritual forces that clashed. We know from the testimony of Rahab (Joshua 2) that the people were aware that God had promised that land to Israel, so that many had mixed feelings about resisting the army of God.

The goal is not just psychological analysis, but adults do explore the story on a more deeply personal level than do children. Adults can face the bigger issues of obeying God's clear commands even when we don't understand them, the cost of resisting God's invitations, the 'right' of God to give land to certain people, the place of righteous war, the cost and value of trusting God, etc.

It takes plenty of imaginative thought to come up with physical activities to aid in the teaching of abstract principles. This is not like changing spark plugs in a car where the way to teach is to demonstrate and then watch students do it in stages until they can confidently do it correctly and completely. Some spiritual processes take place in a logical order, so key words displayed on sheets of paper can be given to a group of people who would then shuffle their positions at the front of the room to put those stages of spiritual development (or whatever) in the proper order. Or if there are levels of intensity of temptation or joy (or whatever), those could be similarly arrayed and sorted. Adults can enjoy such "kid stuff" too. Occasionally.

For the teacher, the painful part of adding such learning games is that they take away precious time from teaching more of the important subject matter. There is a balance between content and absorption, so teachers must look beyond mere time of presentation of more information. The total process involves both teaching and learning.

VISUALIZING OUR TEACHING

We noted earlier that some people are visual learners. That is, their primary input for learning is to SEE things. Their minds want to construct pictures and diagrams that show how ideas fit together or clash, not just fancy ways to make lists.

We can sometimes make diagrams that simplify our thoughts about complex processes. When I taught Basic Doctrine in our Bible college in Brazil I came up with a series of cartoon diagrams (since I am no artist) to relate regeneration and justification, or to illustrate the stages of the adoption process in Romans 8. In our circle of churches in Brazil I was well known for using visual aids in preaching, especially for youth groups. Spiritual truth floods in through the eye gate as well as the ear gate. When they come together there is powerful impact on the memory.

> ➤ One of our students lived in a simple apartment off campus, and sat outside studying for an exam in my Doctrine class. A young neighbor boy saw the cartoons he was studying and asked about them. So the seminary student took a stick and scratched the cartoon in the ground, explaining it as he went along just as I had in

class on the blackboard. He led that boy to faith in Christ! So the method of learning became a method of teaching. It worked! He could do that elsewhere.

Think about how students can SEE your message as well as HEAR it. We don't have smellavision to bring all the senses into play, but there might be occasions for making a point with aromas that accompany the principle. Some simple artifacts from the historical context of a Bible story help convey the reality of it all.

We will dedicate a later chapter to the uses of the computer in our teaching, and will return to this rich toolbox.

STORYTELLING

Good stories illustrate a principle, and tend to remain in the students' minds longer than the simple statement of principle. You can keep an index of useful stories that you run across in your reading like we described for illustrations. Your own experiences will prompt students to relate similar situations from their lives. You can also make up stories like Jesus did as vehicles for truth.

Dr. Bruce Seymour grew up in Africa where storytelling is a primary form of communicating cultural features. His research revealed six basic reasons to use stories in teaching.

1. **To explain the unusual.** The story can feature ideas or behavior pertinent to the point of the teaching, within a familiar cultural setting.
2. **To teach important things.** Written lessons may be true but they are not as memorable or human as stories.
3. **To make things easier to remember.** We organize and store life events in story form, like video clips of reality.

4. **To help solve problems.** The life settings of stories are familiar, so the solutions tested in them suggest ways to approach real life problems.

5. **To help create identity and community.** The similarity of the story characters and the listeners allows a sense of commonality in social interactions within community. "Stories are intrinsically relational" (p. 30) as listeners observe a few people like themselves deal with needs.

6. **To allow us to share the experiences of others.** We learn from how others dealt with problems, participating by observing, and growing by vicarious experience (Seymour 2007, 24ff).

Well-structured stories normally have three phases. The **setting** establishes context and identifies a problem within that familiar territory. Then there is **tension** or tragedy threatening tranquility or life itself. Finally there is **resolution** as solutions are proposed and applied. Sometimes the story ends without resolution so the listener is led to a conclusion that is the point of the whole story. That is a form of discovery learning, with its enhanced impact because the listener solved the dilemma.

The parables that Jesus told were simple and direct, built on familiar contexts, and leading to a conclusion that was often painful. But hearers carried the stories home and discussed them so the force of the story finally hit the target. Again, a parable is a story with one point that sticks.

When composing a story, define the desired conclusion first. Describe a familiar setting, and create a dilemma that will be resolved by applying the principle being illustrated, and keep it brief and colorful. Touch several of the senses. Include the emotions of the moment in your retelling. It is powerful.

All of our teaching is purposeful. It is DESIGNED for impact on the mind and the conscience. It brings to life a biblical concept that is worth teaching. Enjoy it all!

HOMEWORK

Who ever heard of homework in Sunday School? Well, we don't have specific assignments that they are to turn in, but we can create some anticipation in those who are really plugged into the study series. The lack of homework assignments and tests is a measure of the lack of serious accountability. You can't flunk out of Sunday school! When we invite everyone to come to our class we also expect different responses.

Here are some suggestions for HOMEWORK ASSIGNMENTS.

> ➢ During this week, read Ephesians chapter 4 and think about 3 or 4 ways that we display our "new man" out in society.
> ➢ Keep an eye out for common things that can be an object lesson on planning ahead (or whatever you will talk about next week).
> ➢ Work on memorizing this key verse this week. Since we use different versions we'll ask some of you to recite the verse as found in your favorite Bible.
> ➢ After class, ask one member whose family lost a loved one last year to take 3 minutes to describe how God's comfort was a reality for them, or whatever lessons came to mind. (Make it easy for them to say, "No, thanks" if that is clearly awkward for them.)
> ➢ "Next week we will study the final 10 verses of this chapter, so read through it and count the ways we can honor God on our job" (or whatever the passage

applications would be). We will ask for your input.

> Be sure to include the homework in your lesson plan, even if we don't expect (m)any to actually do the work. We can repeat the idea until a few catch on and find it helpful when class time comes about.

Try this one to scare people awake. "Next week we will have a final exam over the entire Gospel of Luke to see how well you have comprehended our study." Such a daring approach is also scary to teachers. We know that if all the students flunk the final exam, the teacher has failed. Ouch!

I did prepare a "Final Exam on Ephesians" at the conclusion of our long study in our ABF class. People gasped. It was really a review of the key ideas of Ephesians, framed as questions. We might have taken an entire class period to discuss our way through the full page of questions. But we did not, due to scheduled events in the church calendar. So it was a take-home review that had value for those who wanted to relive those classes we enjoyed. Try it.

8

PEDAGOGY: Teaching Children

The word "pedagogy" tells us that it means "leading children." It is a mashup of two Greek words for "child" and "lead." In our common usage it has referred to the broader range of the entire teaching-learning process regardless of age. In recent decades adult education has become a specialty as we soon see. For our purposes we take a look at teaching children as a quite distinct process from that of teaching adults.

Children are not simply small adults. There are appropriate ways to teach children that are quite different in form than what appeals to adults. Childhood is all about growth. We can observe the areas of growth in the boy Jesus in Luke 2:40 and 52. As a normal young human being, Jesus grew intellectually, physically, spiritually, and socially. He developed in all the ways we expect to observe in all Sunday school classes. Our efforts are not only in the spiritual dimension, but integrate and prioritize all aspects of growth. Even as we focus on growth that is Godward, it is one element of children's health.

Teachers in both secular and religious education have long distinguished **three domains of learning** so we can address each in appropriate ways.

➤ The **COGNITIVE DOMAIN** deals with knowledge, facts, and stated principles. This is the information level, what we KNOW. In Bible teaching it deals with the content of the Bible, its stories and commands and all else.

➤ The **AFFECTIVE DOMAIN** expresses emotion, feeling, and motivation. In Bible teaching it is the aroused desire to obey Scripture, to enjoy it, feel conviction, love, etc. This deals with how we FEEL about what we know.

➤ The **FUNCTIONAL DOMAIN** simply indicates activity related to the facts and feelings that stream to students in a learning environment. In Bible teaching this is about a variety of physical activities about Bible stories and commands. It can include acting out the stories in classroom dramas, or learning activities such as sorting the books of the Bible into proper order, or putting into practice the real commands of the Bible in daily life. This is how we ACT on what we know and feel. This is commonly designated the Psychomotor Domain.

One of the major differences between teaching children, the Pedagogy we survey here, and teaching adults, the Andragogy we meet in the next lesson, is in how these domains balance each other in the total learning experience. Think about:

1. How many IDEAS can I cram into a lesson before it gets to dense to be helpful? Adults absorb more than children do, taking larger 'bites' of information. We want to include more and more teaching than some can digest and put to use. Be patient.

2. To what degree are these people SELF-MOTIVATING? Will they enjoy and embrace it all, or need to be prodded along a bit more? Adults should drive ahead for the reasons they find compelling, while children may need to be urged along since the teaching content may not seem very useful to them.

3. What can we DO together to help students process the principles or ideas we discussed? Children need more movement, and adults need less, but both benefit from activity that turns information into lifestyle.

We do not intend to squeeze a college course in Elementary Ed into a single chapter. So we can suggest principles that can be applied in a variety of ways for the benefit of the children. Keep your target in view: **Lead these children to desire to know and lovingly obey the Bible.** Everything works together to realize that primary objective of this particular study.

1. REACH

You as the teacher want to connect with each student. The rapport you seek involves trust and confidence. You want each student to report at home, "I like my teacher!" That is a dream, and a healthy one, but it takes time to become a reality. We can resist the natural impulse to favor some students by promoting a purposely diverse classroom atmosphere in all dimensions. Every student is welcomed equally and warmly.

2. READ

In your lesson plan (You are thinking, "My what?" You lay out your approach for major segments of your class period, either on paper or in your mind. Write it out.) you have certain truths you will present in the next class. That knowledge content is the main purpose for the class. They see that the idea comes from the Bible so it is part of God's plan for them.

I say "read," but know it will be read and spoken and presented several times in different forms. By the end of class each student should "know" (and be able to use) a few new facts and principles. You know they will not sit still for a 30-minute lecture, so your key principle may be stated in a couple of minutes and restated often through the course of class.

3. REINFORCE

Children learn by repetition. You have a key Bible verse for them to memorize, and a story that puts that principle in a life setting that is familiar to them. You show how that key idea is a good thing for them. You model it for them from within your own experiences. You may have a game time in which that key principle comes into play. Children need to be active.

Notice the attention span of your group of children. That can vary with the age and social maturity of the children. You will find that certain learning activities can be sustained for 3 to 4 minutes, some for 5-7 minutes, and some for 10 minutes or longer when they arouse that curiosity and creativity that bubble within them. Relate their energy to their learning!

Keep them moving from one activity to another. After your main story you might have three or four activity centers where smaller groups interact. You as the teacher know their limits.

4. REACT

You ask the children what they have observed of that idea. They can be prompted to recite the key verse of the lesson, or help one another to get it word perfect and then recite in unison. What do they think about that idea?

How would they explain it to their little brothers or their congregation of dollies at home? Children participate by nature. They become a part of what they learn. They stimulate each other to learn. Their final exam is the rest of their lives, so we want the key principles we teach to be integrated in life.

5. RESET

How does this verse and its principle change them? What should they do differently because of it? How is Jesus pleased if they act that way? How do parents or friends respond? Will they be better people for obeying the verse? What changes?

The reset can also involve returning the learning environment to order. Toys and books may have been pulled out in dazzling arrays of learning joy. Now it is time to restore the original order of the classroom to be clean and ready for the next class. Messiness is wonderful when it is a dynamic part of progress, but when the job is done the clutter gets put away. Reset.

Children learn that every learning experience is just part of a broader spectrum of life experiences as they grow. It is exciting to learn one new thing. Hit it again.

6. REVIEW

The class concludes with congratulations for all as they recite their verse. Once again they hear the few major points of your lesson as it concludes. They have something to share at home – and maybe a picture or some other handiwork for the refrigerator. They can tell the story at home as parents are encouraged to review the little lessons one more time. Each time a child processes the new bit of knowledge it is driven more deeply into his or her memory and lifestyle. It moves from RAM to ROM in their little computer brains for permanent accessibility as needed.

Begin your next class with a review of the key verse and a request for one sentence that explains the principle. They remember!

WHO IS A "CHILD"?

Within the Bible there are several terms for children in reference to specific phases of life. Many deal with age groups, while some describe relationships.

OLD TESTAMENT TERMS

Age groups in the Old Testament are described by nine words that are more flexible than the following Greek terms. The two most used terms specify the range of children and then youth, though there is some overlap. Age was a social concept more related to obedience to the Mosaic Law and the family than to mere chronological age.

NEW TESTAMENT TERMS

Greek societal structures shaped the terms used in various epochs of life. Each word invites our varied approaches to our teaching.

> - **Paidíon** gives us the *ped-* part of pedagogy. A group of such nouns and verbs related to children indicate instruction, or discipline, or *from childhood* (when upbringing was needed). These are young, dependent children with no distinct age boundary, as the normal word for children. Jesus insisted that the *little children* have access to Him, Luke 18:16.
> - **Brefos** is a helpless infant, used of those just following or even preceding birth. It is never used in teaching contexts.
> - **Nepios** is a baby, one still lacking full abilities of speech. This small child or minor is spiritually immature and still feeding on milk, Hebrews 5:13. In verb form this word indicates childish speechless behavior, 1Cor 14:20

about our non-expression of evil impulses.

> ***Uíos*** (pronounced HWEE-os) means "son" in familial and legal status senses. In Greek, as in later Roman, society a father could designate his legal heirs at any time he felt they were ready. So the legal term for "adoption" as used in the NT is really "placement as a son" with all attendant privileges and responsibilities. This was normally done at puberty, similar to how the Jewish *Bar Mitzvah* invested formal sonship on a "son of the Commandments."

When we look at Acts 16:30-34, wondering which age groups are baptized, we find NO age-related terms within the phrase, *he and all his* v.33 (KJV). The reference to the jailkeeper's *house* naturally included the principal couple and their dependents, younger and older. It could also include domestic servants. The text makes clear that the promise of salvation v.31, the speaking of the Word of God v.32, and the act of baptism v.33, were all-inclusive. Any children still living with a father old enough to be entrusted with the supervision of the prison would be old enough to comprehend the message, believe, and be baptized in the biblical order of such things. This was not a young couple. No babies are indicated.

AGE GROUPS FOR CHILDREN IN SUNDAY SCHOOL

In designing Sunday school instruction, several age groupings have come to be standard descriptors of the stages. Each age group has characteristics that call for instruction designed for their learning styles and levels of comprehension.

Cradle Roll, Ages 0 to 2

Cradle roll ministry is essential infant care. The teaching is not so much theological content but the demonstration of loving care in a safe place away from home. In many ways it models parenting, and integrates the spiritual environment of home and church. Diaper changing stations are in full view of fellow workers, but not the public.

Cradle Roll workers seek to influence whole families to become an integral part of the church as they build relationships with the parents. There may be home visits for sharing the gospel or for helping with tensions in home situations.

Nursery, Ages 3 to 6, Preschoolers

An important dimension of both Cradle Roll and Nursery is safety. Whether parents have grown up in that church or are first-time visitors, they know their precious babies are being cared for by competent, conscientious people. The parents can focus on the worship service and Sunday school classes in peace. In this key sense it is a ministry to the parents.

They appreciate churches that have **high standards** for training childcare workers and a system in place for calling the parents in times of need. The children are released only to those who brought them. Leaders in children's work must be aware of their obligations to observe and report any type of sexual abuse. The childcare facilities are open to the view of other workers in those departments, and entry doors are "Dutch doors" with the top half always open.

Preschoolers develop rapidly in physical and intellectual aspects of life. They recognize love and hate, learn to play cooperatively, can share or can withhold toys for themselves. Attitudes are learned through experience as teachers guide them through the maze of early maturation. Teachers are well aware that all of those cute, lovable children were born as sinners, and see that inborn fallenness begin to manifest itself in their relationships with other children, their teachers, and with their family members.

Preschoolers begin to contain and self-direct their own attitudes as part of growing up. They know what it means to be a loving friend, or an angry threat. They learn to honor and love God as the ultimate model of generosity and love, even when they experience little of that in dysfunctional homes. They know who models 'good' and 'bad' living.

One danger with impressionable young children is pressing them toward "asking Jesus into their hearts" with very limited knowledge of what that means. Many young children have truly believed unto salvation at such early ages, including our own children. But some make a profession of trust in Christ but lack a clear sense of reality. They can end up being inoculated against true conversion by having a light 'case' of Christianity that they get over all too soon.

Teaching materials for these young children focus on pictures, either printed or as pictures they color to go along with Bible stories that are told in a simple form. They can be encouraged to tell the story to family members while showing the pictures. They learn by teaching.

Primaries, grades 1 to 3

Once children begin school their universe expands rapidly. They begin to explore and explain 'what' and 'why.' Keep in mind that some young children keep asking "why?" because it always gets a response from others.

Primary age children love to be active in spurts. Activities can be planned to alternate physical and restful engagement for their short attention spans. On TV and video programs or games the scenery changes every few seconds. We cannot duplicate that in Sunday school, but are aware that we compete with constant change in other parts of their world.

By this age, children love stories and can differentiate true from fantasy stories. They deal with concrete reality so the more abstract concepts of God, sin, forgiveness, kindness, etc., are explained and illustrated in concrete terms. Notions of right and wrong are already in mind and are strengthened by examples and consistent admonitions. Children from widely differing conditions and standards at home will learn to obey and appreciate their teacher's standards consistently applied. They are learning what behavior fits which context.

Now in school, these children are dealing with identity and social acceptance outside the family. The loving acceptance within the Sunday school class gives a sense of security as well as conformity to proper social relationships with healthy give-and-take with different people.

We can talk about God freely without trying to define Him theologically. He is always present; He loves and cares for children; Jesus welcomed little children to come to Him; He does not care what color skin people have, and created them all to be friends. This is a learning time about good and evil, and for the present we presume their good will toward God without pressure. The Holy Spirit will awaken a sense of sin in His own way and time.

Primaries are engaged in all the key domains of learning: head, heart, and hand. They are best approached through stories, those that abound in the Bible, and those that bring biblical principles to life.

Vacation Bible School focuses on Primaries and Juniors while others who are younger and older benefit as well. It is a time of concentrated study that can cement concepts of God's loving authority in the Bible and the Church.

Juniors: 4th to 6th grade

These preteen years are vitally important in the continuing development of children. Their sense of who they are in . society is taking shape, and will soon be challenged in junior high school. Will they (and others around them) regard them as among "the dumb ones" or "the smart ones?" "The good kids" or "the bad kids?"

"Challenge" may be a great summary term for Juniors. They are aware of their growth in several key areas:

> **PHYSICALLY** they are competitive, want to be noticed as successful or even the best. Their energy abounds. They want to be active on worthwhile things, and love the outdoors. They may be into early phases of the war of hormones as they notice and enjoy differences between boys and girls, especially as our society flaunts sexuality. They are all just waking up to each other.

> **INTELLECTUALLY** they are inquisitive, beginning to realize how much there is to learn and how little of it they know. They can accept the challenge of gaining serious knowledge of the Bible if they work at it. They become aware of the reality of history, not merely as old dates and events, but as their own family roots.

> **SOCIALLY** they are tasting and testing authority. They tend to have a sense of fairness at a level of seeing whose turn it is or who got a bigger piece of cake, but that will develop into sensitivity about justice on the public level. They are aware of racial issues and want to test equality in friendships. They know to accept responsibility, or how to avoid it.

Juniors are thinkers. They are ready to understand doctrine at appropriate levels: basic concepts about God, Jesus Christ, the Holy Spirit, the Bible, the Church, prayer, Christian character as the result of their relationship with God, their biblical place in the home, and even their responsibility to reach out to their community and world with God's good news.

Juniors are quite ready to understand the gospel of Christ and to make a knowledgeable decision to call upon Christ as their only hope for salvation. Why is baptism important? Now is the best time in their lives to begin regular memorization of Bible verses as an internal resource for victory.

CHILDREN are the future of the church. So they are treasured both as our own offspring and as the next generation of God's instruments in this fallen world. These will soon venture into the most dangerous decade of their lives, from age 15 to 25.

GROWTH IN DECISION MAKING

An essential ingredient in maturity is the ability to make moral decisions that help rather than hinder spiritual development. And desire inner conviction and initiative that makes those key decisions their own. There is a time for just following "what Dad and Mom would expect of me." A big part of maturing is valuing those principles within our own discerning hearts.

We presume a learning environment that honors the Bible as the final expression of God's design for mankind, and that it is realized when learners allow Jesus Christ within them to live out His own life in theirs. So the moral and ethical development of both children and adults is not just learning more rules but allowing the New Ruler to be at home ("abide") in them.

In our own Sunday schools we freely draw our standards from

what is taught in the Bible or is in harmony with the Bible when found in other sources. We quietly accept the authority of God and of His Word in our lives. Children may or may not find this basic principle reinforced at home, so Christian teachers are laying a vital foundation for the entire lifespan of these precious little ones.

As children move into their teen years they face the prospect of making decisions for themselves. ALL people make a transition from following parental guidelines to being self-guided from within. Your teaching in their tender and receptive years will facilitate their transition into self-guided lifestyle in harmony with God's Word. That is the desire of every Sunday school teacher and of most parents.

But not all of the children in your class benefit from Christian parents who take the Bible seriously. Secular schools have become more blatantly anti-biblical in terms of moral authority. Strong investment now will pay great dividends in the development of character that is guided by biblical principles in later life.

Teaching children is far more complex a process than can be described in these few pages. The appropriate managing of the ideas in class is complicated by the difficulties of managing any group of children. Our focus here is primarily on teaching adults or young adults so the very brevity of our summary of Pedagogy is not ignorance but focus on a different target.

9

ANDRAGOGY: TEACHING ADULTS

Here is a secret you already knew: Adults are NOT just large children. Children and adults learn differently, so we want to have in mind some principles of how adults [prefer to] learn. This is not just different exercises, so much as the attitude that we as teachers bring to the classroom. Keep in mind that YOU are adult learners even as you read this lesson. Does it fit you?

The teaching of children is Pedagogy. The teaching of adults is **ANDRAGOGY**. *Andros* is a form of a Greek word for "man" that stresses the virility and strength associated with adulthood. Some robots are called "androids," or "in man-form." So, in our adult Bible classes we will have some fitting concepts rattling around in the back of our minds. We should review this list every so often.

One key principle we easily forget when we teach the Bible (and related subjects) is that we are not just teaching the content of the Bible. We are teaching the Bible to PEOPLE. Our aim is not to convey mere knowledge, but a sense of the value, authority, and usefulness of the Word of God in their lives as individuals, families, and citizens. We are not so much teaching new facts as developing new learners who will develop habits of learning and obeying the Bible for a lifetime! Your being a teacher is really an investment in servants of Christ.

In this lesson we draw from the works of Dr. Malcomb Knowles who organized such teaching principles into recognizable form and called it Andragogy back in the 1960s. It was aimed at trainers in vocational schools, but that is sort of what we do in adult Sunday school as well. We are not training professional ministers, but helping any adult Christians to apply biblical truth to their personal growth and ministry. We are learning with them, not just teaching as if we knew it all.

BASIC PRINCIPLES AND APPLICATIONS OF ANDRAGOGY

These ten principles apply to all adult learning situations from college to prison to vocational training to graduate school to Sunday school. Try each one on for size.

1. ADULT LEARNERS ARE FREE.

Adults voluntarily come for instruction and growth, without obligation or pressure except from within themselves. Only their own will keeps them under instruction, and they may freely leave when the training is not useful or interesting to them. They are free to think, "Who needs ABF?" and stay home. They are also free to move to a different class with a better fit or content of greater interest to them. So we strive to keep it practical and valuable for our fellow-students. We want them to want to come regularly.

2. ADULT LEARNERS CHOOSE WHAT TO LEARN.

Maturity and experience bring perspective on what is still needed in the life of an adult. Curriculum designers propose plans for learners, but those plans are accepted or rejected or adapted by the adult learners. These students will request or seek what they feel they need and want rather than just take what is offered. They expect a choice even when compelled by other factors (like "All church members ought to study in ABF!") Is ABF worth the effort? [Hint: "YES!"]

Even if we use curriculum from our favorite Christian publisher for our ABF class, or Sunday school or whatever we call it, we have to opt to dive into topics for which our class members feel a need. We do well to offer options to the class, or simply ask what they want to study. Then it depends on the teacher's capacity to develop or find materials suitable for the class members. That is what this TRUSTpages Series is for.

Adults feel in charge of their learning programs. Some will move from class to class as they find topics of interest being taught. Or, some ladies prefer to be in an all-ladies class. That is a good thing, much as you want folks to loyally stay in YOUR class. They continue to learn in a chosen environment.

3. ADULT LEARNERS WANT LIFE-RELATED STUDY.

For some adults, their life needs information about art history, but most simply ignore the availability of such good stuff. We get the catalog of adult courses and lectures at local colleges or the library, and look for what WE want for our own improvement. We select among church programs, special conferences, radio programs, recorded lectures, and online courses. Since each life is different, there is no "one size fits all" approach. Adults want to invest time in subject matter that is useful to their personal lives. ASK what they want to study. If it is something you have not really studied then get to work. Or, you might invite another teacher with such expertise for a few weeks while you sit as a student yourself.

4. ADULT LEARNERS WANT TO PARTICIPATE IN LEARNING.

The experience that adults bring to class is a resource to be valued and used in discussions, research questions for specialists, asking questions. Each one is an expert in some things that others are not, and would like to contribute from their point of view. We seek ways to draw students into the teaching process as they process the information together. It takes more time, but gets driven in more deeply. As you talk in class, try to sense who among the students has an experience or area of knowledge that he or she would love to share with the others. Try to create some teaching times for such participation. They will love it. It is more their class when they get to give something to each other.

5. ADULT LEARNERS EXPECT MORE EMPHASIS ON LEARNING THAN ON TEACHING.

The focus is the needs of the student not the preferences of the facilitator. Agree on objectives, work together toward them. As teachers we can help people learn, but cannot teach them unless they are active participants in the process. So class is more about learning by the students than teaching by teachers. Isn't that the same thing? Not quite. It is all planned around what they need than around what we feel like teaching. Still, the teachers have more perspective on what is really needed, based on their fuller experience and/or training.

6. ADULT LEARNERS EXPECT TO WORK IN AN INFORMAL ENVIRONMENT AMONG PEERS.

Relaxed protocol, snacks, movement, discussion, and variety all contribute to a sense of mutual helping. Unbroken lecturing may give good content, but it alienates adults who expect to discuss, interact, argue, apply and share fitting experiences. In an adult class, all have important insight and experience that becomes an integral part of the overall lesson. Be sure that students know one another's names, and use them. Keep the atmosphere open and warm. Comments by students are not interruptions but a welcome part of the learning process, as long as no one student dominates discussion. Younger adults may enjoy facing each other in a circle, while older adults are accustomed to sitting in rows facing a teacher. Ask what fits.

7. ADULT LEARNERS EXPECT A FACILITATOR IN MUTUAL LEARNING, NOT A MERE EXPERT LECTURER.

Remoteness of teacher from students cancels any effect of the expertise of the teacher. Share experiences, life, feelings, and limitations. And welcome such comments from class members. Learners expect to identify with the teacher as a human person and experienced fellow-learner in the area of study. Our own failures can be tastefully admitted as part of our own learning of biblical principles and common sense wisdom. The adult Sunday school class is not the place for an ivory tower demagogue who knows it all.

8. ADULT LEARNERS EXPECT TO LEARN SERIOUSLY, NOT JUST JUGGLE THEIR MUTUAL IGNORANCE AROUND.

True expertise is rightly expected in the teacher, in some measure. Learners are free, and will leave if the class does not resonate with their reality, respect their contributions, or correspond to their level of general education. If they feel they already know more than the teacher does it may feel like a waste of their time. There is competition for their time. If they move to a different class, be supportive. Know the expectations of your class, including the technical level of content they can handle comfortably. We don't give homework or exams in Sunday school, but should expect to stimulate some serious learning and personal growth.

9. ADULT LEARNERS WORK TOWARD PROBLEM SOLVING IN REAL LIFE SITUATIONS.

Adult education is practical in its nature, undertaken out of a sense of need for improvement in specific areas. Or, in scheduled or perpetual studies, like ABF, studies should lead to useful improvement through knowledge gained. Give tools for problem solving, not just pat answers for some questions. Are others in class learning to study and teach? Share parts of some lessons with some students as fellow-teachers. Some of your best students might start classes of their own as the church grows. Always have a "So what?" section of the lesson that deals with real situations in students' lives.

10. ADULT LEARNERS EXPECT TO BE EVALUATED ON THE BASIS OF PRACTICAL APPLICATION OF NEW KNOWLEDGE, NOT BY MERE GRADES ON INFORMATION.

Our fear of criterion-based public education is not the principle of a criterion basis, but our uncertainty as to who are setting what criteria. The principle is sound when the criteria are appropriate. If we learn to do what was expected, the experience was successful. Since we don't give exams in ABF, the final exam is the rest of life.

So we conclude where we began: adults are not merely larger children. There are principles of adult education that enhance our effectiveness in teaching when we learn and apply them.

ABF is a form of vocational training. It is not about carpentry or cooking or dressmaking, but about living biblically in a social context that does not take the Bible seriously. So students in ABF are the trainees, and they expect to come out of it all as better equipped servants of Christ. Teachers, listen carefully to them as they state what they expect. Out of a church menu (the list of adult classes at the church) they selected YOUR class for their main course. Take their choice seriously and deliver the goods!

Adults are the core of the church membership. Are they better trained for having suffered through your training courses?

MAJOR AGE GROUPS OF ADULTS

We know intuitively that all adults are not the same. They vary by interests, levels of education, family background, social maturity, religious heritage, spiritual maturity and motivation, and other important dimensions. For the purposes of ABF we commonly divide adults by age groups as that commonly reflects the ages of dependent children under their care, if any. When ABF classes are indicated by age limits, those are suggestions rather than legal barriers. People will select their classes by preference and comfort, often following those age brackets.

HOW ARE ADULTS DIFFERENT AS THEY PASS THROUGH PHASES OF LIFE?

YOUNG SINGLE ADULTS.

The most dangerous decade of life follows graduation from high school. Normally 17 or so, these young adults face their four most important decisions.

> **Lordship.** Will they personally embrace the faith of their families as their own faith? Will they continue to be regarded as Christian believers while they grapple with assaults on biblical faith? Will they throw it all away in the name of personal independence? Now is the time to reaffirm the faith in which they have been raised, and

made their other key decisions in light of the Lordship of Christ in their lives. Keep in touch so they don't just drift.

> **Lover.** The second most important decision in life is whom they will marry, if anyone. That will influence more than any other matter they face. This is a key factor in starting their further education in a distinctly Christian college where they are more likely to discover likeminded potential mates. Marriage is the sharing of lives for a lifetime with mutual influence and needs.

> **Lifework.** Major career choices are made in this key decade, particularly as they enter college and choose their major field of study. It is far more than just finding a job, but entering a career that will channel one's energy and strengths in useful ways. Vocational counseling is beyond the scope of this brief study on teacher training.

> **Lifestyle.** In this decade most young adults will adapt to one of several appealing lifestyles governing many dimensions of adult life. Friendships come from their associations in matters of interest, so biblical standards are needed to guide the choices made along these lines.

It is easy to see how adults in this key decade either step up in their involvement in the life and service of the church, or step away from what they perceive as irrelevant to their new independent existence. They NEED vital Bible orientation at this very time of life. Too many leave the church and return a decade later with a spouse and children, and a sense of need for God's guidance, often after being burned.

NEWLYWED ADULTS, first 10 years of family life

Once people marry they take on a totally different sense of

responsibility in life. They learn that decisions have consequences, and that people are important to the balance they need in life. When young children storm into the formerly peaceful household everything changes again. They naturally seek the company of other young couples with similar circumstances. They are often climbers in their chosen career paths and may need to move away to follow that path, but while here they are the high-energy future of the church and key to growth. The Bible study they need is related to family life, relationships, integrity, and parenting. Those are matters that occupy their optimistic energy and attention in their 20s and into their 30s. They know struggle and change are not enemies but stepping stones. These high-energy ABF students are creative and curious. They want to discuss and even argue as they sit in circles and explore new levels of Bible teaching.

While we consider this dynamic age group, let's take some advice about...

WORKING WITH MILLENNIALS

The "millennials" are those born from about 1984 until the end of the 20th century. This burst of population are the children of the Baby Boomers (born 1946-1964), most of whom have only known the digital electronic age. By 2020 those young adults would be roughly 20 to 35 and bringing plenty of changes. They are also called "echo boomers" or "Generation Y."

Do we really need to redesign our traditional Sunday school for every key generation that comes along? Of course we do! Using materials and media from the 1950s or even 1970s would be like speaking a foreign language. How do we teach this group? [Here we adapt great ideas from *A Brief Guide for Teaching Millennial Learners* by J. Bradley Garner (Triangle Publishing, 2007, pp.12-15)]

1. Take time to know the names and life stories of your students. Some of this calls for time outside of class as we interact with them as whole persons with their own unique histories.
2. Try new approaches beyond the old familiar routines. These folks value experimentation, and are risk takers.
3. Always connect lesson content with lifestyle context. Ask "So what?" and "Now what?" along with your sterling information flow.
4. Know how to use teaching technology well. This age group knows it well and is not impressed by bumbling along, either missing out or messing up in media usage.
5. Tell stories. Use narratives that carry principles rather than just stating principles. Stories are the windows that transparently show off truth.
6. Try group projects for learning. Millennials love teamwork. Group discussions can study and present their findings to the class.
7. Expect your students to do well. Set the bar high to challenge them to excellence instead of expecting them to be indifferent to your lessons.
8. Ask more; talk less. Bring probing questions to class to stimulate fruitful discussions and group study. Provide resources for study so they can teach one another.
9. Keep protocol informal. Millennials generally respect fairness in the application of authority. Our authority is the Word, not the teacher.
10. Express your passion! Show that the truth you teach really matters. Cool intellectualism does not have as much impact as really caring about how your subject matter makes a difference in the community and world.

Millennials were raised being told they were always special, and could do whatever they want to do in life. They were given trophies for participation even when they lost (so they thought "So what?" or "Why bother trying hard since it will be given to me anyway. I'm entitled to recognition and favor.) But when they finished school and ventured out into the real world they found it did not work that way. Many were disillusioned with the failure of the world to treat them as they deserved. They had to grow into load-bearing adults overnight. They quickly learned to be optimistic but suspicious.

MARRIED ADULTS IN 30s and 40s

The stable core of the church is these maturing adults, often with growing children. They have settled into their roles in marriage and career. They become the teachers of the younger generation. They realize that Bible knowledge must involve more than excitement and zeal, so they are ready to work on establishing a working knowledge of The Book for their own growth and teaching. They are ready for serious Bible study, including doctrine. They wonder why they are in THIS church instead of THAT church and want to anchor their faith in certainties and reality that matters to them. They are taking on leadership roles and have a sense of mission that will carry them through decades to come.

Still...some of those promising marriages have begun to unravel, and need serious attention. Their idealism was not salted with realism and some resent what their spouses have become. In class they want to participate and share in the teaching, ready to try new formats.

FAMILY ADULTS IN 50s and 60s

The serious leaders and decision-makers provide stability, and are models for the newlywed generation. Some among them have also run after a second childhood and torn up their solemn promises of faithfulness to family and church to chase other priorities. They remember school as listening to their teachers, sitting in rows, and being orderly. They wonder why the young adults don't fit in at church.

SENIOR ADULTS, retired

Veteran Christians have moved through the earlier stages rather successfully. They have memories of 'the good old days' when church was like church and not like a youth rally. Some grumble, and most come to accept that times have changed as the Bible has not changed, and the work goes on with or without them. Church is all the more important to them now as their primary social gathering. They need to be productive.

Bible study is more of a reflection of their past, and many have been teachers for decades, now just enjoying being stirred and reminded. They need love and attention, especially after some have lost their spouses. Bible study is a source of comfort in familiar truth, affirmed again and again as they anticipate Heaven. They also remember school as sitting in rows and listening politely, but have a lot to share of insights and experiences related to the Bible passages. Social times are important to them.

Seniors have time on their hands and often volunteer. Most towns have organizations that serve the community in many areas of need. They have a few professionals who guide a large number of volunteers. Such service is an expression of the compassion of the church members, not a conflict, whether or not it is a religious organization.

> ➢ There are literacy training centers, GED mentoring programs, ESL teaching for recent immigrants, crisis

pregnancy centers, and other programs that can use whatever skills the Senior Citizens have. Churches also have services in nursing homes, jails, military service centers, and other such places where the church reaches into the world. Turn those seniors loose! It is ministry to *give a cup of cold water* to those with a broad variety of needs. Some seniors were executives in their career days, and may have a lot to offer to the church and ministry organizations nearby in areas of strategic planning and restructuring for efficiency.

Adults are the core of the church membership. Are they better trained for having suffered through your training courses?

10

HOW CAN WE USE COMPUTERS?

I got my first computer in 1984. It revolutionized my studies and eventually my teaching. But however valuable a tool may be, it is only a tool that enhances (or frustrates) the creativity of the craftsman who uses it. Let nobody dare to say, "I don't have a computer so I cannot be a good teacher." Many of the greatest books were written before there were typewriters, or even the printing press.

The ABF teacher is a person with mind and heart geared to teaching the Word of God and the life it builds. Tools enhance those efforts, but the heart and mind make the teacher.

The computer provides five primary aids to the ABF teacher where we will focus attention. These are 1) access to research assets on the Internet, 2) the writing of our lessons, 3) the storing of our lessons, 4) the presentation of the lessons in class, and 5) record keeping.

HOW did we ever function without them? But when we did not have computers we did not know what we were missing, any more than we can drool with anticipation over whatever else might be developed in coming decades. We work with what we have, as always, and adapt to new tools that come along.

1. ACCESS TO RESEARCH ASSETS

We do not intend to attempt a complete webliography of the Bible study materials that abound online. That changes every month, so no such list is ever final. We can explore the kinds of materials that can be found with simple searches so the ABF teacher will find more than he or she ever imagined or would be able to use. It still comes down to YOU preparing a lesson for YOUR collection of students. Many of the materials are free, and some involve some cost.

I keep a file folder on my computer desktop with several Bible study resources. I can dip into those readily, but I still enjoy having open books on my desk which I can scan and compare more readily there than online. My most frequently used is www.BibleGateway.com when I need to find the reference for a biblical phrase that is rattling around my head without an address. That **concordance** function works in many versions in many languages. Other "books" on that "shelf" include a Bible encyclopedia, interlinear original language texts, lexicons, and collections of maps.

Bible study materials abound online, in English and increasingly in other major languages. You will come to collect your own favorite works that work for you. Your colleagues will have suggestions for you, and you for them. Networking is valuable for resource sharing. Here are some categories.

BIBLE STUDY LESSONS. Your favorite search engine will lead you to more Bible study material than you can handle. Some is readily adaptable to your teaching, and some is poisoned with unbiblical doctrine. Know your sources.

MAPS. Relating Bible story events to real places helps to cement the sense of historical reality. Remember how much time it takes to move from one place to another. Remember that in ancient maps the sense of "up" was not north but east as they were oriented toward the Orient, the sunrise. And notice that in the Bible one always goes UP to Jerusalem and DOWN from there. It is both the capital city for God's people and temple, and set upon a high hill, Mt. Zion. I have even used current maps in class that I pulled from Google Maps. Mountains don't move. I always give due credit to sources and watch for copyright restrictions if publication is in view beyond that one class.

BIBLICAL REFERENCE BOOKS.

> **COMMENTARIES.** Some commentators go verse-by-verse while others deal with paragraphs. You will find your own favorites in time.
> **LANGUAGE ANALYSIS WORKS** if you have training in biblical languages. Look for the more precise meaning of key words if they carry a lesson. Don't just recite grammar without some value. The tenses of verbs are important as the indicate the sequence of preparation, action (sporadic or continuous), and aftermath (completed or continuing).
> **BIBLE VERSIONS.** Comparing phrasing in class helps when we get more precise meanings. Otherwise don't casually spend a lot of time without benefit.
> **SERMON SERIES** in audio files or text files. Your favorite preacher will have some insight that you can quote or adapt into your own words. But listening to sermons is time-consuming.

ILLUSTRATIONS. You can keep a computer file of your own helpful illustrations for lessons as a table. Only do this if you will be able to find the stories on specific topics later. The law of inverse filing still works: Time spent on careful and specific filing or labeling material reduces the time it takes to access those stories when you need them. Learn how to run a SEARCH of your computer-filed documents, and try to remember the titles you gave to your files, or unusual words within them.

Keep your written comments brief, and you can expand on them when you tell the stories or use the object lessons in class. There are collections of sermon or lesson illustrations online, but your own stories or observations are always best. In class you can ask people for their experiences with class topics. Remember their best stories to add to your collection. As your collection grows you can sharpen the focus of your TOPIC words to keep illustrations accessible.

You can set up a table in landscape format with four columns:

- ➢ Topic (a one-word key for sorting)
- ➢ Scripture reference (if tied to one key verse)
- ➢ Body of the story (in the widest column)
- ➢ Date used (to avoid repetition with the same group).

If you are planning to use a computer to facilitate your teaching efforts, remember that the computer does not analyze the passages, parse the verbs, or write the lessons. YOU do that. The computer is just a fancier pencil.

2. WRITING YOUR LESSON

It can take a while to undergo one essential "conversion" from writing out a lesson and then keyboarding it into the computer to doing all your work at the keyboard. You will find that it is far simpler to compose at the keyboard and then edit your work. Even if you type slowly you will find it gives time to rethink each sentence and word as you compose your lesson.

One of the biggest gains in computer use is that you can work on lessons and readily edit and change them later on. You can 'scribble' rough ideas in an idea file and come back to that later for development. You can ask the computer to check your spelling and grammar if that is not part of your DNA.

It is easy to move sentences around, change words, shift paragraphs, and abbreviate to make it fit within the template for a lesson. But what you write is saved and ready for your next phase of preparation. Use the advantages of word processing and grow with usage.

I have a standard template for lessons that I have used for many years. A blank copy is set up to print the two pages back-to-back and folded to be a 4-page handout. For each lesson series I can fix a template for the series with the title of the series, date, Bible passage in a heading. For each lesson in preparation I do a "save as" with the number and brief title for that lesson. Those are saved in a file as they are prepared.

When I am developing a lesson for class I tend to write it within the template for that lesson. This keeps me within practical time limits for one class period. I do some editing to crunch it into that space, but in class I talk around the notes instead of just reading them. Students can follow along, write notes, etc.

I can rough out a lesson with just headings and then fill them in, in any order. You too can rewrite whatever you want to change. Some parts that you have clearly in mind can be written in their space, while parts that call for more study can wait a few days. Do an early rough draft and add to it as time allows. Let it rest and come back to it as something new. Then give it a final touchup, proofread it, and print it. Copy it for class! I like to prepare drafts of lessons two or three weeks ahead so when busy days pile up I am not pressured to 'get that lesson done' right away. (That happens too.)

3. STORAGE OF RESOURCES AND YOUR WORKS

Today's computers have massive storage memories. Bible study works are essentially all text, so they call for small storage space compared to color movies or games. You can set up your own array of files in your Documents section, depending on what you store. Here is what I do.

TEACHING NOTES. Under DOCUMENTS I have a major file called ABF LESSONS. Under that I have categories of lesson series that have accumulated over the past 20 years and more. So, under PENTATEUCH I have files for GENESIS, EXODUS, etc. and for TOPICAL Studies. Under PAULINE EPISTLES I have files for Corinthians1, Corinthians2, Ephesians, etc. The computer culture does not have a function for sorting in canonical order, so I just leave them in alfa order. Or, it is easy to add a letter to the beginning of each filename to sort them in canonical order making your 'aa Romans' to come before your 'ab Corinthians1' instead of way after it. Your choice.

Each lesson series file folder (Exodus) then has standard items:

- ➤ A **schedule** of classes for that book or topic
- ➤ A **template** which I copy with a 'save as' for each specific lesson with its number and title, like 'Rev 211.' I begin with 201 since the stupid computer doesn't distinguish single-digit or two-digit numbers, so it would arrange #10 right after #1 instead of after #9. But it can easily arrange 201 then 202 then 203, etc. The heading has the series title, date, lesson number, and Scripture text reference in constant format.

➢ The lesson series follows with a **file for each lesson** with number and lesson title: Isa607 ch19-23 Hammer the Enemy and Isa608 ch24-27 Isaiah's Apocalypse, etc. My practice is to prepare a handout which is one sheet of paper, printed on both sides, so with four pages of text when folded. Those are my teaching notes.

➢ **Supplementary materials**, maps, others' notes, etc. I may come up with class ideas at odd moments so they get scribbled down before they evaporate from my mind, That file is a junk box where I toss in anything that might prove helpful. Once the series is done, some of that is deleted or moved to its permanent home.

SERMONS. Most ABF teachers are not preachers, so just skip this part if it does not fit. Again, I have a master file for SERMONS with categories under it. As a data nerd I keep a table of all preaching occasions, called PREACHINGLOG. It lists the sermon or lesson number, date, a title or topic, place and occasion. The table can be sorted by date or place or any of the columns, but is normally in date order from newest to oldest. This goes back 50 years for me, and got started when I realized (too late) that I had preached the same message twice in a row at one church I was helping occasionally. Ooops!

When you have prepared a lesson on your computer it is saved forever in whatever filing order you devise. You will not lose that scrap of paper that had your lesson ideas until a windy day carried it unto the ends of the earth.

4. LESSON PRESENTATION

TEACHING NOTES. In the classroom, I have not normally used the computer, but am well aware of the ways an on-site computer can be a quite powerful aid to presentation. I have preferred handouts that the students can take home.

I described my own practice in preparing my teaching notes as handouts. They get all that I have. In this approach to teaching there is no difference between a teacher's 'quarterly' and the student 'quarterly.' They have it all. We can take time to discuss questions that arise since I know the students (who really want it) have the teaching material to take with them even if I hurry through parts of it..

Every lesson gets finished in class, even if I rush through the final parts. In my preparation phase I sometimes realize that the Scripture passage before us merits more than one class period. So at that stage prior to class I divide it and start preparing a next lesson to complete it. That is much better than leaving part of that lesson to be completed next time. You never catch up.

I have even given out copies of suitable lessons as gospel tracts.

ARTISTIC AIDS. For years I used an overhead projector for notes in class and so kept a clip file of frames and pictures to highlight what I outlined on the transparency. That is obsolete now, and I am no artist. In Brazil, and in other overseas places, I was careful to use only visual aids that my students could reproduce for their own use. If expensive projectors were not available, I used common poster board and "atomic pens" for my visual aids so they would do the same in their teaching.

If you use the computer for teaching there are many styles of lettering, clip files of pictures, and templates for your diagrams. Visually interesting slides of essential sentences and outlines can take the place of handouts if students are not using them to read later at home.

PROJECTED VISUAL AIDS. Any office suite of computer software will have something equivalent to PowerPoint® or Keynote® for projecting your teaching notes. Outline your key ideas in the "slides" along with key quotes, Bible verses, maps, and suitable pictures. Be sure that the type size is large enough for people in the back row to see clearly. Have any pictures you use really enhance the text rather than distract from it. This requires that you follow the order of the slides in how you prepared your presentation.

Visual aids create interest. But they also facilitate learning by providing an outline of the material being taught. The slides are normally summaries of what you have prepared for the lesson. Some students will want to take handouts home rather than just copying summaries from the screen. But the writing process gives students another form of processing the material in their minds. The computer software offers a printout of the slides with space for students' notes. That may be a welcome option for serious students.

There are great opportunities to inject some humor from suitable cartoons. Always give credit to artists by including their names as you cut out cartoons for copying or scanning.

5. RECORD KEEPING

A final area where computers help in education is the maintaining of information of attendance and grading.

> ➢ **ATTENDANCE** is recorded by a simple entry of each student's presence or absence. No calculations are normally done for ABF apart from possible adding up the count of students week by week. The presence of class members is normally noted by a volunteer class secretary for the church's own records. But you as a

teacher can follow this closely with your own records.

➢ **GRADES** are best entered in a SPREADSHEET which is tailored to fit the demands of the course. The major requirements for a course like this are weighted in the final reckoning of a grade. Raw data can be entered as testing and papers come along, and a formula calculates the final number grade. None of that applies to ABF since we have no assignments, tests, or firm requirements. All of the activities are voluntary. Nobody can flunk out of Sunday school.

The computer is your friend, IF you have one and know how to use it. If you do not have a computer, just carry on as you have been doing. Plenty of good work is done without technological help from a machine. It is merely a machine. It is not smarter than you are, only faster. (And its memory is probably better.)

YOU the teacher are the real instrument of God's working in that classroom. Go for it!

11

WHAT ELSE DOES OUR CLASS DO TOGETHER?

An adult Bible class is more than a weekly class. It is a social unit within the larger structure of the church that can express its own togetherness in venues other than the one classroom for the one hour every week. We really get to know one another in informal situations apart from the rush of the scheduled classes and services at church. Large churches can enjoy having several adult classes with their own identities. In small churches the adult class IS the church core, so some of the group activities suggested here may not apply directly.

The ABF class is not the whole church, so we do not seek to duplicate the overall array of its ministries. Our ABF class is ONE of many elements in the outreach and inreach efforts of the church as a whole. We are not the primary worship and preaching service for the congregation as a whole. We do not take the place of small group ministries for Bible study since they involve a dozen or so people to develop spiritual intimacy with a few people. ABF is not designed as a support group for dealing with problem issues like our focus groups can do.

In the church's overall plan for developing healthy Christians it is good to think in terms of each believer participating in...

➢ the principal worship/preaching services,

➢ an ABF class, and

➢ one small group study or ministry/service function.

We are sternly warned in Hebrews 10:25 of *not forsaking the assembling of ourselves together*. Father knows how much we really need each other as a resource for growth. We may think it is simply a meeting we go to, but our church gatherings are a way of recharging our spiritual batteries. We need to be in the total congregation for singing aloud the praises of God and hearing together the exposition and application of Scripture. We see joyful faces, and we are one of those joyful faces that others see. We are proclaiming that for this hour this is the most important place in the world for us to be!

We also need the detailed study of the Bible by books and by doctrines as we teach one another from our own experiences. It really is a "school" so we should take AFB seriously as a constant refresher course on the Christian life.

We need to be involved in outreach ministry with others of our fellowship. That can be one of the focus groups to help those with special needs, or a small group study cell where intimacy aids our ministering to one another. Find ways to give as well as to receive of Bible teaching and living.

SMALL BIBLE STUDY GROUPS.

A "small group" should be small to allow intimacy in how we express our feelings and needs. In a small group everyone knows everyone and can call them by name. That suggests between 8 and 12 persons to be a true "small group." Once larger it begins to focus as a small large group with less free interaction. It is easy for group discussions to devolve into two discussions among the six persons sitting near each other.

We've been in one another's homes and circumstances. When together, everyone can look everyone else in the eyes and speak heart-to-heart. This is valuable fellowship for the nature of the fellowship even more than for the subject matter of our Bible studies. People need to know they are valued, and are missed if they do not participate.

ABF SOCIAL GATHERINGS

There is more to shared life than just Bible study, wonderful as that is. We influence each other in the things we do together. What are some other occasions for getting together? When we plan class activities we always begin by looking at the church calendar. We work within, not against, the overall ministries of the church so we do not want to compete with all-church plans where we want our class members to participate.

PLANNED PARTIES. Each ABF class is free to plan and hold its own social gatherings without feeling obligated to invite all of the church to join them. These may be seasonal, or birthdays, or whatever else we wish to celebrate together. This could be at a home or public park as desired. Younger families decide whether or not to include small children.

SHARED MEALS. Eating together is an expression of common trust and values. We mix and eat and enjoy one another's cuisine and company in a variety of styles of a meal. Sometimes the class can go out together, have a carry-in supper, a picnic, or any combination of people and food while conscious of the Lord's presence and blessing. There may or may not be a devotional talk or study. Sometimes we are just being Family.

CONCERTS. At least once each summer our small group goes together to a Friday night concert by our fine town band. We have no structure other than sitting together and enjoying (most of) the music. We are together. We see other friends in the crowd sitting around the park and go greet them, but we sit with our group as a group. An ABF class can do the same, even better yet that such concerts are free and each family brings its own seating, or blankets.

WORK PROJECTS. When class members work together they are in fellowship, whether or not it is a function of that ABF class. When the pastor asks for volunteers to help to serve a meal for the church, or the town, we step up to help. We encourage that in our announcements in class. Some of our class may go on a missions trip, so we encourage them, pray for them, hear their report on return. All of us were involved in it. People from our church are involved in starting new churches in or near our big city, so when our class members visit to encourage them, they speak for us, and we value their reports on how it went. All of us are involved in it.

ABF SERVICE PROJECTS

How can we help a family from our class that is in need? Sometimes one class member is ill or absent for a while and we all can step in to help with some of their normal household work, inside or outside. The important thing is that they know we all stand with them in a time of need. It expresses love, even when punctuated by sweat.

Think about service opportunities by the whole church that are affected by our ABF class.

> ➤ **TEACHING.** We gladly surrender our ABF students to teach a different class, whether for adults, teens, or children. We have not lost them; we have trained them.

➢ **STUDENT MINISTRY.** Our teens are the future of our church so we value them and invest in them. When our ABF students help out in ministries for teens and children at other times we salute and thank them.

➢ **PRAISE TEAMS.** Music teams have become a key part of our worship experience. So when musicians arrive late or leave early for ministry in a service during our class I thank them for serving. They are not interrupting but are serving in a different room. Thank you!

➢ **SERVICE MINISTRIES.** Our people volunteer in worthy Christian service organizations right in our town, and we count that as part of what our church contributes to outreach. Some help in women's clinics for counseling and adoption help, or in service to the needy. We also help in secular services with tutoring, clean-up projects, helping families with work projects, and visiting those who are in jail.

➢ **FOCUS MINISTRIES.** Some ministries of the church deal with specific areas of need for churchfolks and for others from the community. Leaders need to have the appropriate training or experience to lead such groups. Those support groups are not directed to the entire church but to those who seek such specific help.

Dealing with specific problem issues such as marital stresses, addiction problems, anger management, cessation of smoking, or managing personal finances may limit the size of the groups. They call for confidentiality about problems discussed and even who is present. But in ABF we recognize and encourage those special ministries and those who lead them.

We want to avoid piling many responsibilities on the few who are eager to serve. When those few have the good sense to say

"No, thank you" to additional opportunities, they open doors of opportunity for new people be drawn into more active participation in the vital life of the church. Participation in spiritual exercise develops good spiritual muscles for heavier tasks in the future. Focus on drawing more young adults into teaching activity rather than allowing them to drift along in passive inactivity. The older church members have a history of faithful service, but they started out much younger and grew. It is time for other young adults to step up and BE the ones who carry the load of church ministries.

Saying "No, thank you" also helps avoid the mistaken notion that the church calendar is more important than the family. We do not measure spiritual maturity by the number of hours per week we are away from family activities "doing God's work." In truth, family activities ARE God's work for parents as they lead the tiny congregations entrusted to them. Stay balanced. When church leaders spend eight days a week away in church doings we too often find that their children feel robbed of parents or feel they are less important than meetings.

We support the pastors when they spend normal time with their families. That is part of their ministry to us, and to their families as they show biblical balance of responsibilities. Their own tiny congregations are their own primary mission field.

12

THE EVOLUTION OF ONE TEACHER (Me)

Let me tell a bit of my own story. Why do I dare write such a book as this, or expect you to be reading it?

I did not grow up in a family of teachers, so my school on schooling began as yours did, as a student, and not a particularly good one – at first. My university degree is in Mechanical Engineering, like my father, and my mother was a research chemist. None of this is background for a teacher of teachers. Yes, I'm aware of the old saying, "Those who cannot do, teach. Those who cannot teach well, teach teachers." (Don't believe it for a moment.)

COLLEGE DAYS

Engineering gives an analytical bent, a focus on organizing resources to solve real problems. My professional interest was originally in Fluidics. That is a form of machine control circuitry using compressed air going through logic devices that are arrayed for decision making. Such circuitry is programmed for environments that are not friendly to electronics.

While a university student, however, I was called by God to foreign missionary service, so my time in engineering was limited to about the seven years that it took for Doris and me to get to our mission field. Some of that work included developing computer programs for complex calculations we had done by hand, or by calculator. That was 1969 when a "computer" was a multi-story building full of cables and vacuum tubes. But it was programming of a different sort than my dreams of Fluidics. Later, in seminary, I was a graduate assistant in an undergrad class, tasting college from the other side of the desk. That got less frightening as it went on.

SEMINARY DAZE

In seminary the focus was on learning content: what the Bible says, and means, and intends. But there was virtually nothing in that whole M.Div. program on communicating that message apart from Homiletics – how to prepare and deliver sermons. There were courses on Christian Education but I only took one course on Curriculum Planning, mostly comparing published adult quarterlies. That was helpful, but it hardly prepared me for my first serious teaching assignment a few years later.

During my seminary years we were part of a brand new church where we got plenty of ministry practice as sort of an informal internship. Doris and I led a group of junior children in the enjoyable 4th to 6th-grade range, and I taught an adult Sunday School class that even included some of my future seminary profs. I had a teacher's quarterly so many of the tough decisions were made for me. I accepted the fact that I could not teach some of them new information, but could *stir up their pure minds by way of remembrance* as Peter advised. It was a positive beginning.

ON THE MISSION FIELD

Once we landed in Brazil in 1970 and later completed our formal course in Portuguese, I knew I did not know how to speak well enough to be teaching, but also knew I did not know how to teach a class. I needed to organize material, see where it fit among similar courses, gather the material that was the substance of the course, find textbooks, understand the capabilities of my students, plan a semester, and even put together the lesson plan (whatever that was) for my first class. And that was my job now, as a seminary teacher. I thought, "I should have learned how to do this!"

So, if I now work readily with all of those elements, you can be assured that I learned them all the hard way. The trial and error method produces plenty of trials and errors. But those are great teachers if we respond positively to them, and I did. The engineer in me kicked in and allowed me to analyze the need, propose a solution, try it out, adjust this and that, and try again. Those iterations, or repeated attempts with minor improvements, paid off. I got so the planning and structuring of a new course was a real delight.

By our third year I contributed an article to a Brazilian magazine on Theological Education on *Planning a New Course*. It struck a positive chord and was republished a few years later, enjoyed by an editor with a Ph.D. in Education. The substance of that article is embedded in some of Chapters 6 and 7 in this present book. When we learn things the hard way we learn them thoroughly. For some people that all comes naturally. But I had to slug it out line by line. One advantage of that was that I learned the drill well. I devised my own procedures and checklists that I later learned were in line with sound professional methodology.

Somehow I blithely assumed that my missionary colleagues on the faculty were all doing all those things. Dream on! I was later named Academic Dean, so I said that by the second week of each semester I wanted a copy of their course plan for the semester to keep on file, and by the end of the semester, a copy of their rough daily lesson plans. The Brazilian faculty members all said "fine" and turned it in. That had been part of their university training and was accepted as normal routine for any school. But the American faculty members regarded me as an alien from Mars and muttered polite things that masked their thoughts more like, "Who does he think he is?" I was still the new kid on the block with too many radical ideas.

My first extra-curricular project in Brazil had been the organization of a distance learning program for our seminary. Back in the 1970s such programs were wedded with programed textbooks so I was into yet another form of programming related to training. In the seminary I taught a course in *Theological Education by Extension* using a programed textbook I had written so each of our graduates could be a certified leader of an extension center wherever they scattered in the vast Amazon Valley. In time we had just shy of 100 students in 14 centers, only two of which were led by us foreign missionaries. The logistics and distances later killed that program, but it was an education in itself. That also got me into a lot more reading about educational methodology and planning in both English and Portuguese. I was evolving into a teacher of teachers. Who would have guessed it?

During our first furlough I was eager to get back into academic harness so I enrolled in a Master's program in Communications at a Christian college close by. One course that I took was just what I had needed all along, *Learning System Design*, with a textbook of that same title. It was like Heaven! It was an engineering approach (well, systems approach) to the planning and preparation of a course and entire curriculum. It sort of put flesh and skin on the bones I had roughly assembled myself. That was THE most useful course I ever took anywhere.

When we returned to Brazil in 1975 I found I had been named Director of the seminary, so that brought on a totally different major project. I had long felt that we were running an Americanoid school in Brazil when it ought to have become a Brazilian school in Brazil. We had Strong Brazilian faculty members who were quite capable of running the seminary, even as we foreigners could continue to teach and cooperate as invited. So I was visiting Brazilian high schools to see how they were structured administratively. They had someone who was the "Academic Coordinator" whose job it was to oversee the semester plans and lesson plans, along with enforcing the grading system and other logistics that kept the place running sort of smoothly. It was fun to invade the Faculty of Education at the University of Amazonas to ask basic questions they must have enjoyed for their simplicity.

I got into examining issues like faculty pay levels, accreditation, and legal matters for schools. We had to modify constitutions of the seminary and of our mission's Brazilian entity to allow a Brazilian executive council to serve as the school board instead of the missionaries of our region, all while keeping peace with our colleagues (some of whom had moved away by then).

So I got introduced to yet another dimension of schooling, when all I wanted was to be a teacher and pour myself into the students. They would become the next generation of pastors, national and even foreign missionaries, and other Christian workers, men and women.

Even when I pastored a church, it was really to train the seminary students who worked with me. One of them was called as their pastor when he and his bride graduated from seminary, and remained there for years afterward. We find our sense of success in the success of our successors!

The final months of that second term were really tough as Doris and I wondered if God wanted us to return to Brazil or if He had something else for our future. We did not know, and could not talk about it. Long story short, after we returned to the States the president of the mission called to ask me to pray about coming into the administration of the mission. We prayed, talked with many others, weighed options, took a hard look at spiritual gifts, agonized over a tough decision. We concluded that it was God's leading and accepted the position.

BACK IN THE STATES

In 1980, after completing the M.A. and taking a first doctoral class, I entered the offices of Baptist Mid-Missions in Cleveland, Ohio, as an administrator rather than as a missionary after twelve years. I would be the Candidate Administrator in charge of recruiting, evaluating, and training new missionary recruits for our work in over 60 nations of the world. I would be discipling new missionaries! But my travels to many campuses of colleges and seminaries in the States led to new invitations to teach modular courses in Missiology, my main field of study. Once again I was teaching, and enjoying it immensely.

In the church we joined in Ohio I taught a Sunday School class of high schoolers, and then of adults. My travels meant I needed always to have a co-teacher so I was constantly training someone to take my place. That sounds like the approach I had in Brazil.

But my occasional teaching here and there meant I was always designing a new class, now more as Master's and Doctoral level classes after I graduated again in 1985. I even got to develop a graduate course in *Training National Leaders* to teach in Asia since the future of missionary work is in the hands of those who are coming to Christ all over the world. By 1990 more than half of the international mission workers around the world were non-North Americans. The receiving churches were maturing as sending churches, just as God planned it from the beginning of the Church.

My final major project at the mission headquarters was to develop an online continuing education program for our missionaries. I was custom-tailored for that project even though it demanded my learning a pile of new dimensions of the teaching-learning processes. This was yet another type of programing. The four years we invested in that project involved learning course management software, writing a ton of instructional material for missionaries' personal growth and professional development, and promoting a program to help missionaries who were already too busy.

Meanwhile, we had moved to Medina, Ohio, in 1989. The co-teacher I had trained was quite able to carry on that class on his own. We joined our current church, First Baptist Church, where I was soon a co-teacher in an adult class of what was now to be called ABF, Adult Bible Fellowship. For the first time I was not working within a quarterly system in which book or doctrinal studies had to be completed in 13 weeks or 26 weeks. The other guy left the class in my hands and moved away.

For more than 20 years I have enjoyed that class immensely and have learned a great deal in the open-ended discussions we have enjoyed. I developed the system of handouts of one sheet folded over, so with four small pages. A few years ago one of the (really sharp) guys in class asked, "Is there any way other teachers can get ahold of this good stuff?" A bell rang in my head since I had already gotten into digital self-publishing of other teaching notes.

So, thanks to Mark's simple question, we have about 20 books of ABF classnotes as a resource for adult or teen teachers in a variety of settings. These TRUSTpages Series books can be useful for Bible studies in campus ministry, prison, military, camps, and youth classes. I retired at the end of 2009 so that class is now the highlight of my week. My dear wife Doris has been a vital part of it all, and has managed to not get weary of having the same teacher for much of her adult life.

My modular course teaching dwindled with time and changes in schools, in part because there are more capable teachers available now. Some of them were in my classes as they trained for the ministry. We go in cycles.

When I was invited to teach a class on *Principles of Teaching* this little book sort of erupted out of my prepared mind and soul. Now you know why.

This little Postlude offers my personal thanks to God for the many who taught me, including those I have been blessed to teach.

A BIBLIOGRAPHY on Principles of Bible Teaching for Adults

Some of the works noted are more in the field of Educational Psychology than teaching principles, foundational to classroom work and designed for school teachers. Some relate to Theological Education for training pastors and other ministry or education professionals. Most are by Christian authors while some are secular in focus. We learned from ALL of these.

ARTHUR, Kay
2001 *How to Study Your Bible.* Eugene OR: harvest House Publishers. A noted Bible teacher gives excellent training in personal Bible study methods, mostly inductive.
BARLOW, Daniel Lenox
1985 *Educational Psychology: The Teaching-Learning Process.* Chicago: Moody Press. This outstanding Christian textbook covers the whole field of theory and practice for teachers, and theological educators do need such training. It is more geared to general education than ministry training, but offers practical help vitally needed by ministry trainers, adaptable for overseas.
DRAVES, William A.
1997 *Teaching Online.* 2nd Edition. LERN. (ISBN 1-57722-003-X) This is a fine, down-to-earth introduction to methodology in adult education. It is geared to secular schools like vocational classes and junior colleges, but is very practical for missionaries teaching in seminaries around the world as well as for Sunday School teachers of adults, young adults and teenagers at all levels of maturity.

FEE, Gordon D. and STUART, Douglas

    1982   *How To Read the Bible for All Its Worth.* Grand Rapids MI: Zondervan/Academie Books. A couple of seminary scholars offer this fine "Guide to Understanding the Bible" with a focus on the various kinds (*genre*) of literature used in the Bible and the particular interpretive principles to be applied to each one. Written for laymen, the users of the Bible. Useful.

FORD, Leroy

    1991   *A Curriculum Design Manual for Theological Education, A Learning Outcomes Focus.* Nashville: Broadman Press. Here is the ideal cookbook on how to design a curriculum and prepare specific courses, very helpful after the conceptual homework has been completed, and cultural sensitivity developed.

GANGEL, Kenneth O. and HENDRICKS, Howard G., editors

    1988   *Christian Educator's Handbook on Teaching, The.* Wheaton IL: Victor Books / Scripture Press. An encyclopedia on Christian teaching for church and home from the faculty of Dallas Seminary has invaluable impact on teaching in cross-cultural settings

HAKES, J. Edward, Editor

    1964   *An Introduction to Evangelical Christian Education.* Chicago: Moody Press. This fine collection of 32 essays by leading Evangelical educators of the time surveys the field with thoroughness and competence. In its day it was the standard textbook in the field, still valuable.

HENDRICKS, Howard G. and HENDRICKS, William D.

    1991   *Living By the Book.* Chicago: Moody Press. The father and son team well known as Bible teachers present their menu for personal and shared Bible study under the headings Observation, Interpretation, and Application. Very useful.

KNOWLES, Malcolm S.

    1980   *Modern Practice of Adult Education, The: From Pedagogy to Andragogy.* Revised and Updated. New York: Cambridge, the Adult Education Company. This foundational text on adult education is must reading for theological educators since adults learn in ways significantly different from children. Much technical detail here is beyond the needs of Sunday schools, but essential for all adult teachers.

SEYMOUR, D. Bruce
2007   ***Creating Stories That Connect.*** Grand Rapids MI: Kregel Academic. A pastor/counsellor/MK teaches us to compose stories that illustrate the application of biblical principles.

SMALLMAN, William H.
2001   ***Able to Teach Others Also.*** Pasadena CA: Mandate Press /William Carey Library. The revised dissertation focuses on the nationalization of theological education along with a broader array of educational principles for seminaries.

TATE, Marcia L.
2004   ***"Sit & Get" Won't Grow Dendrites.*** Corwin Press/Sage. A seasoned trainer of teachers presents an excellent selection of teaching methods that work with students in public schools – and should work in Sunday school.

YOUNT, William R.
1996   ***Created to Learn: A Christian Teacher's Intro to Educational Psychology.*** Nashville: Broadman & Holman. This became the new standard textbook in Ed Psych for Christian teachers, practical for missionary teachers in seminaries and for Sunday schools as well.

CHECK OUT OTHER RESOURCES IN THIS **TRUSTpages** Series (with Number of lessons):

GENESIS 1-11: ORIGINS (26)   GENESIS 12-50 (18)

EXODUS: Follow the Cloud (27 lessons)

EZRA & NEHEMIAH: Building & Battling. (22)

LUKE: Jesus as God's Ideal Man. (68 Lessons)

ACTS: Up, Down, & Out. (40 Lessons)

1CORINTHIANS: Order in the church. (32)

2CORINTHIANS: A Heart for Ministry. (21)

PHILIPPIANS: Rejoicing in Adversity. (22)

THESSALONIANS: Jesus is Coming! (22)

HEBREWS: Christ the Superior One. (22)

LETTERS of JAMES & JOHN (16 & 19)

PATTERNS FROM PETER (& JUDE) (39)

DIMENSIONS OF GRACE. (16 Lessons)

CATHOLICISM FOR BAPTISTS. (14 Lessons)

More are currently in preparation. Check Amazon.Com and enter 'Bill Smallman' to see the full list of current titles. You can enter 'William Smallman' to see a further list of sound Bible study topics of interest to you. Or, see http://TRUSTpages.biz to see them all.

Made in the USA
Monee, IL
24 June 2020